THE ENVOI MESSAGES

Louis Phillips

BROADWAY PLAY PUBLISHING INC
New York
www.broadwayplaypublishing.com
info@broadwayplaypublishing.com

THE ENVOI MESSAGES
© Copyright 1985 Louis Phillips

All rights reserved. This work is fully protected under the copyright laws of the United States of America. No part of this publication may be photocopied, reproduced, stored in a retrieval system, or transmitted, in any form or by any means, electronic, mechanical, recording, or otherwise, without the prior permission of the publisher. Additional copies of this play are available from the publisher.

Written permission is required for live performance of any sort. This includes readings, cuttings, scenes, and excerpts. For amateur and stock performances, please contact Broadway Play Publishing Inc. For all other rights please contact the author c/o B P P I.

Cover art by Dixon Scott
First printing: September 1985
I S B N: 978-0-88145-031-6
Book design: Marie Donovan
Set in Baskerville by L & F Technical Composition,
  Lakeland, FL

For Pat

"*For every mile the feet go
the heart goes nine*"

Foreword

The problem with Louis Phillips is that he is an obscure poet and brilliant playwright. In most ordinary people, one or the other of these blessings is possible—not both.

I can't be utterly positive, but I *think* this is what happens when you participate with him by reading the bloody, besmirched pages: you read along and mutter to yourself that this man is insane. How dare he—and what the hell is this all about?

Then the house falls in on your head. The impact of a moment of pathos or tragedy or sheer hilarity grows out of the morass of wild prose and poetic abstraction. Now you've got—you've got it! Life is so tawdry and barren—and yet it has beauty and hope and it's been set down just as you've felt it a million times over.

Well, Mr. Phillips. ... one day you may be recompensed for the pain inflicted by those who have not yet understood what you are about. It doesn't even matter whether you understand it yourself. One day—soon—your far-outness will make the bridge to the mass and we will recognize a brand new literary Elvis. Is that a good thing? I don't know. I just hope you keep skipping rope inside your world of fantasy from the Marx Brothers to Western Union.

I wonder. ... are you a humorist or a seriousist?

STANLEY KRAMER

THE ENVOI MESSAGES premiered at the Indiana Repertory Theater on 15 January 1975, with the following cast:

BLYTHE DONNER	Brenda Currin
WINTHROP HALL	Maxwell Glanville
FIRST APACHE	Henry Kaimu Bal
SECOND APACHE	Robert Machray
HAWK WOMAN	Delia Elizabeth Hattendorf
FIRST CANNIBAL	Jeffrey V. Thompson
ELIZABETH DONNER	Loretta Yoder
MATTIE TRUERIDGE	Rosanna Carter
ALBERT DONNER	Robert Scogin
CHAUFFEUR	Jeffery V. Thompson
MARK BALLANGER	Bernard Kates
MRS. HORACE DESMOND	Linda Selman
OFFICER MILTON	Lou Malandra
CHESS SHIRE	Robert Machray
XT-N-R4	Barry Cullison
PRIVATE MASON	Barry Cullison
PHANTOM GORDON	Maxwell Glanville
CHIEF DANCING FOX	Robert Scogin
REFEREE	Lou Malandra
ANNOUNCER	Bernard Kates
MAN WITH A ROPE	Jack L. Davis
SPEECH MAKER	Delia Elizabeth Hattendorf
MOON MONROE	Henry Kaimu Bal
CROWD	Duncan Larsen, Robert Machray, Loretta Yoder

Characters

By calling upon the full resources of the supporting actors to double and triple in roles, *The Envoi Messages* may be performed by a cast of four women and six men:

BLYTHE DONNER	ALBERT DONNER
WINTHROP HALL	OFFICER MILTON
APACHE NO. 1	REFEREE
WRESTLER NO. 1	MARK BALLANGER
CHESS SHIRE (astronaut)	MATTIE TRUERIDGE
MOON MONROE	
APACHE NO. 2	MRS. HORACE DESMOND
WRESTLER NO. 2	HAWK WOMAN
CHAUFFEUR	ELIZABETH DONNER
PRIVATE MASON	SPEECH MAKER
XT-N-R4 (robot)	

ACT ONE

Scene One

(*SCENE: At the opening of the play, the stage is dominated by a large electric sign that blinks on and off—WESTERN UNION. Descending from each end of the sign are two wooden lattice-work structures supporting vines and roses. Underneath the center of the sign is a large white door with perhaps a few steps leading to it. Hanging from the doorknob is another sign—this time a cardboard one that reads—MESSENGER WANTED. However, the electric sign should dominate the scene and should resemble no other sign in existence.*)

(*Standing downstage from the sign and door is* BLYTHE DONNER, *a boyish-looking girl of thirteen or fourteen years of age. Dressed in a boy's blue suit with a cap upon her head, she stands facing the sign and holding her English bicycle, the one precious possession she has. It is not new though and has seen much use. She slowly approaches the sign and then parks her bicycle. Before going inside she makes certain that her bicycle is carefully locked.*)

(*As* BLYTHE *approaches the sign, a large wooden desk is rolled in at stage right.* MR. WINTHROP HALL, *who has been in charge of this particular branch for a year or so, enters and takes his place behind the desk. He is a large black man of Irish extraction, with white hair and a kindly face, though he often attempts to hide his gentleness with gruffness. The fact that he is from Ireland gives him some advantage in dealing with the whites of the small town in which he works, though his position and his "foreignness" tend to isolate him slightly from most people in the community.*)

(*Upstage from the desk a coat rack, holding the official uniform of Western Union messengers, is flown in.* BLYTHE *removes the bicycle clips from her trousers and then removes the sign from the door. She enters with determination.*)

(*The year is 1934.*)

(WINTHROP *continues writing.* BLYTHE *clears her throat to gain attention.*)

WINTHROP HALL: What can I do for you, lad?

BLYTHE: I've come to see about the job, sir ... (*Shows him the sign*) The sign on the door says you're looking for someone to deliver messages.

WINTHROP: The sign's not on the door now.

BLYTHE: (*Not taking the hint.*) No sir. (*No reply*) If you need somebody, I know this city like the back of my hand.

WINTHROP: You do, huh? What's the back of your hand look like, kid?

BLYTHE: (*Seriously*) Well, the metacarpus or the body of the hand, has five bones, while my fingers, or the phalanges as they are technically referred to, contain 14 bones. The 14 bones are ...

WINTHROP: You a wise guy or something?

BLYTHE: No, sir. I just thought ...

WINTHROP: It's getting so that everybody who comes in here lately is a wise guy. I tell them they can send ten words for seventy-five cents, and they come up with words like metapsychosis ... Who needs it, huh? I've got better things to do with my life than look up words in the dictionary for a bunch of wise-guys.

BLYTHE: I have my own bicycle, which my father bought for me before he left, and I'm free every afternoon after two o'clock, and on Saturdays and Sundays, including Saturday and Sunday night if you need me, except of course I can't work on Sunday morning because Momma thinks I have to go to church to get religion because Poppa didn't have any, but then I don't think you are open on Sunday, are you?

WINTHROP: Do you always talk that fast?

BLYTHE: If I were delivering messages, I would speak slowly and distinctly, just try me ... and I can sing: (*Sings quickly*) Happy birthday to you, Happy birthday to you, Happy birthday,

Scene One

dear Winston, Happy birthday to you. (*And adds, speaking*) And many happy returns to the day.

WINTHROP: Who's Winston?

BLYTHE: I don't know. It's just a name that came to mind. Winston Ticonderoga is the full name.

WINTHROP: Sit down and take a load off you feet, kid.

BLYTHE: (*Taking chair*) Thank you. Now when do I start? ... My bike's right outside. That is if you need any urgent messages delivered right away.

WINTHROP: Start what?

BLYTHE: The job.

WINTHROP: I haven't hired you yet, kid. Now take it easy. The world's not going anywhere. It was here before you were born and it will be here long after you've departed.

BLYTHE: I'm not going anywhere.

WINTHROP: I was afraid of that. (WINTHROP *removes some employment forms from his desk drawer.*) O.K., kid, what's your name?

BLYTHE: Blythe Donner, which everybody says sounds like Santa Claus's reindeer. I live at 19 and ½ Uneeda Lane with my mother, and we're alone because my father ran off with some floozy and my mother has tuber ...

WINTHROP: Kid, I don't want you life story. Just answer the questions. (*Mutters to himself*) Floozy ... (*Shakes his head*) Now how old are you?

BLYTHE: Thirteen, but I'm old for my age.

WINTHROP: I'm old for my age too ... That make two of us ... What's "Happy Birthday" going to sound like when your singing voice changes?

BLYTHE: I don't think my voice is going to change ... I'm a girl.

WINTHROP: (*Nodding sadly*) You're a girl. (*He replaces the paper and pen into the desk drawer. Closes it.*)

BLYTHE: What did you do that for? Don't you have any more questions for me? ... I have lots more answers.

WINTHROP: I bet you do.

BLYTHE: I can ride faster than any of the boys in this town, and I can do the job, and what's more I'm smarter than Reedy Miller, even if Mrs. Cuyler gives him all A's just because he's her pet.

WINTHROP: Don't call us. We'll call you.

BLYTHE: You can't do this to me! It's not fair! It's discrimination!

WINTHROP: Look, Blight ...

BLYTHE: Blythe!

WINTHROP: What would your mother think if I set you out at night alone into some of the worse neighborhoods God ever conceived ... I mean maybe you just think that nice people get telegrams ...

BLYTHE: (*Furious to the point of tears.*) I can take care of myself.

WINTHROP: Just suppose some night you're delivering a telegram, and this guy is home all by himself, and suppose he's been drinking or something, and suppose he invites you into his apartment ... I can't spend my time worrying about that ...

BLYTHE: What's he going to invite me into his apartment for? ... Men! You all think alike ... You know what you are, don't you?

WINTHROP: What?

BLYTHE: You're a ... You're ... You're a thick-headed Irishman, that's what you are.

WINTHROP: I'm just thinking about your poor old mother who'll be sitting up every night worrying about you.

BLYTHE: Don't boys have mothers to worry about them?

WINTHROP: It's different.

SCENE ONE

BLYTHE: How?

WINTHROP: You're bending the sign.

BLYTHE: If you don't give me this job, I'm going to take you to court. I'm going to sue you for discrimination ... My uncle, the state's attorney, will be down here so fast that it'll make your head swim.

WINTHROP: Your uncle who?

BLYTHE: The state's attorney. You know who the state's attorney is, don't you?

WINTHROP: (*Standing up*) You're bluffing.

BLYTHE: Try me. I'll show you I won't be pushed around. I won't be discriminated against. I'll put Western Union out of business that's what I'll do ... I came here in good faith to apply for this job. And if girls can't apply then you should say so on your sign, so I don't waste my time coming down here. In fact you're going to pay me for the time it took for me to come down here.

WINTHROP: Hold your horses, will ya? ... Now you tell me something. You don't care about going into the rough neighborhoods, into the bars, into the whore ... into the houses where the floozies are?

BLYTHE: You pay me and I'll go.

WINTHROP: Girly, you talk big ...

BLYTHE: Don't girly me, mister.

WINTHROP: (*Thinks*) All right ... You see the uniform hanging there ... Try the jacket and cap on. It's got to fit you. It's one of the requirements for the job, because Western Union doesn't have the money to buy new uniforms everytime somebody leaves ...

BLYTHE: It'll fit.(BLYTHE *tries on the jacket and the cap, both of which are too large for her small frame. Still she refuses to give in.*) I'll grow into it in a couple of days.

WINTHROP: (*Amused*) Try a couple of years.

BLYTHE: My mother can shorten the sleeves and I have my own cap.

WINTHROP: You've got to wear the company's cap.

BLYTHE: Who says?

WINTHROP: Now if you want this job as badly as you say you do ... (*Opens the drawer and removes the papers and pen.*) Miss Donner, then I suggest you follow the rules ... Now you take this booklet home with you and read it carefully, and report back here at three o'clock sharp tomorrow afternoon.

BLYTHE: I have the job then? I'm not going to come back here for nothing.

WINTHROP: Unless I retire. And at this moment I'm thinking about it quite seriously.

BLYTHE: Shall I take the uniform home with me?

WINTHROP: As a hostage? ... Take it, take it. But if you're one minute late, so help me ...

BLYTHE: I won't be late ... I was champion time-teller in first grade ... Boy, wait until I tell Reedy Miller. Won't he turn green with envy.

(*Lights out, except for the large sign outside. It blinks on and off through absolute darkness.*)

Scene Two

(*Dream Sequence No. 1:* BLYTHE *is centerstage. She sits proudly on her bicycle and pedals furiously. From offstage come the sounds of Indian drums and strange electronic humming. On her head she wears the Western Union uniform and the pockets of her suit are stuffed with telegrams.*)

BLYTHE: If I do not reach the Hawk Woman in time, all the soldiers will be massacred ... Scalped in retaliation by the savage Apache whose name means "ENEMY" ... Onward faithful bicycle, two-wheeled three-speed God ... Into the valley of death ... Neither rain nor snow nor sleet nor dread of night will stay this faithful messenger from her course ...

Scene Two

(*Indian sounds erupt. The huge, savage masks appear through the darkness, then two* APACHE *warriors who carry bow and arrows. As a rain of arrows clatters to the stage,* BLYTHE *opens one of the two baskets on her bicycle and removes a black umbrella. As she opens it up to protect herself from the arrows, a single arrow sticks up from the fabric.*)

APACHE NO. 1: (*Simple announcement to the audience*) Little messenger survives the rain of arrows ...

APACHE NO. 2: Little messenger delivers words from the hawks (*There is the howling of wolves.*)

APACHE NO. 1: Little messenger survives the howling of the wolves.

BLYTHE: I must not look back, I must not look back, I must not look back.

APACHE NO. 1: Little messenger rides the silver serpent like a red man ...

APACHE NO. 2: The silver serpent once protected the house of the gods ...

APACHE NO. 1: It is time to speak of the myth of creation ... (*The umbrella floats freely up into the wings.* BLYTHE *outstretches her hands and places her feet upon the handle bars.*)

BLYTHE: Look ma, no hands.

APACHE NO. 2: Before the house of the gods, there was no Apache.

APACHE NO. 1: The long plain of the world had not been conceived. There was no grass nor sea.

APACHE NO. 2: No star dwelt in the darkness.

APACHE NO. 1: No moon lingered over the prairie.

APACHE NO. 2: The God of the Holy Mound created the wild deer.

APACHE NO. 1: The wind was a forest. (*Sound of a fox barking. Perhaps the faces of foxes. Snow begins to fall.*)

APACHE NO. 2: At last the Apache came to tame the wild deer, the wind and the stars ...

APACHE NO. 1: But now the little messenger rides beyond the song of the foxes.

APACHE NO. 2: The God of the Holy Mound allows snow to fall upon her.

APACHE NO. 1: The prairie of stars she rides through is ice.

APACHE NO. 2: Fog saddles the trees for a long ride.

APACHE NO. 1: Somewhere beyond the barking of the fox, the Hawk Woman with round belly waits. (*Sounds of a woman in labor. A buffalo hide is dragged forward by the two* APACHE. *Upon the buffalo hide is the* HAWK WOMAN *who is giving birth.*) God of the Holy Mound, the time of birth approaches.

HAWK WOMAN: Where is my baby ...

APACHE NO. 2: We must not scare the little messenger away. (BLYTHE *dismounts from her bicycle, opens the basket that is attached to the handlebars, and removes a baby wrapped in swaddling clothes.*)

BLYTHE: Hawk woman, from a great distance, I have brought your child. (HAWK WOMAN *takes the child in her arms.*)

APACHE NO. 2: We dance in praise of Western Union ... (*They dance.* BLYTHE *returns to her bicycle. It rears up in cowboy fashion and* BLYTHE *waves her hat over her head.*)

BLYTHE: I'm sorry that I can't stay but I must deliver birthday greetings to General Custer before it is too late ... (*Blood-curdling cry of a white-man.*)

APACHE NO. 1: (*Matter of factly*) So much for the birthday greetings.

(*The* APACHE *and the* HAWK WOMAN *retire.* BLYTHE *begins to pedal furiously. The Indian drums change to drums of Africa. A huge black pot is rolled out. Inside the pot is* WINTHROP HALL, *naked to the waist. The pot is guarded by giant cannibals with human bones through their nostrils and long gold earrings dangling from their ears. They carry huge spears.*)

CANNIBAL NO. 1: Stew again. Every night stew.

Scene Two

CANNIBAL NO. 2: Why can't we eat out like everybody else?

WINTHROP: You're nothing but filthy beasts, boiling a man alive for your own pleasures ...

CANNIBAL NO. 1: When we look at a human being we see only calories ...

CANNIBAL NO. 2: I say prepare the stew. What are we waiting for? (*From offstage there is trumpeting of elephants. Actors dressed in the costumes of monsters enter. At first they are separate monsters but they soon unite to form one animal.*)

CANNIBAL NO. 1: We are waiting for a message from my aunt, Winston Ticonderoga of the Upper Uganda. She is sending us her special recipe for thick-headed Irishman. (BLYTHE *dismounts from her bicycle and mounts the back of the monster.*)

CANNIBAL NO. 2: You know no messenger has ever survived the terrible desert or escaped from the pygmies with the poisoned darts.

CANNIBAL NO. 1: Why, who is this approaching through the clearing?

WINTHROP: I wish you wouldn't talk with your mouth full.

CANNIBAL NO. 2: Why yes, it is our messenger.

BLYTHE: (*The attitude of royalty*) I deliver you the recipe from Winston Ticonderoga ...

CANNIBAL NO. 1: Hey, Joe, you wouldn't have a quarter on you, would you? The smallest I have is a five-dollar bill.

BLYTHE: (*The monster backs up.*) I suggest mayonnaise myself ... (*The monster stretches out upon the stage and the outer skin now forms a bed.* APACHE NO. 1 *crawls out from underneath.*)

APACHE NO. 1: We have attempted all forms of communication ...

CANNIBAL: We have tried drum.

APACHE: Fire and smoke.

CANNIBAL NO. 2: Knots on a rope.

APACHE: Stones piled in intricate formations ...

(MRS. ELIZABETH FARRAR DONNER *enters. She is a frail woman who looks much older than her actual age of forty-five, forty-six. She approaches, dream-like, the bed where* BLYTHE *now lies sleeping.* MRS. DONNER *carries in her hands the Western Union jacket which she has now shortened for her daughter.*)

CANNIBAL: We have used the conch shell as a trumpet ...
(*From offstage, a conch shell is sounded.*)

APACHE: We have reflected sun off the blade of a knife ...

CANNIBAL: We have pounded stones together in the middle of the night.

ELIZABETH DONNER: Blythe, wake up ... You've been calling out in your sleep ... My, you're all covered with sweat ...

BLYTHE: What time is it? Am I late for work?

ELIZABETH DONNER: It's not even light out yet.

BLYTHE: Is my uniform ready? Can I try it on?

ELIZABETH DONNER: Not now ... You better change out of your wet night-clothes.

APACHE: She will ride the light of the stars and the sound of the fox will follow. (APACHE *imitates the sound of the fox.*)

BLYTHE: Momma, is forty-five cents an hour a living wage?

(*Lights out*)

Scene Three

(*Time: Six months later.*)

(*Lights slowly come up on a white porch swing. Sitting on the swing is* MRS. MATTIE TRUERIDGE, *a very old black woman, thin, wrinkled, with white hair. Still she is splendidly strong and wears a faded housedress that is haphazardly buttoned, and upon her feet are*

Scene Three 11

unlaced boots. Next to her on the swing is a large molasses jar, which from time to time she will raise to her mouth. In the distance there is the sound of a harmonica playing, hounds barking or baying at the moon, and every once in a while, an owl hooting in the pine trees. MATTIE *slowly rocks back and forth with a rifle opened across her lap. She sings, half to herself, a lullaby. (See Appendix A.)*)

MATTIE: (*Stops singing*) Is someone out there ... (*Continues singing*) I know there's someone out there. My eyesight may be failing but my nose is still good. (*She sniffs the night air. The sound of a hound barking intensifies. There is the sound of a twig snapping.* MATTIE *closes the barrel of her shotgun and stands up, aiming it.*) Who's there? Who's there? ... Stop, or I'll shoot. (BLYTHE, *dressed in her messenger's uniform, emerges from the darkness.*)

BLYTHE: Don't shoot! ... It's only me.

MATTIE: Who's you?

BLYTHE: Western Union. (MATTIE, *not lowering the shotgun, considers the answer.*)

MATTIE: Is all of you Western Union or just some of you?

BLYTHE: I have a message for you.

MATTIE: What's a white girl doin' out this way?

BLYTHE: I've come all the way from town ... I think it's a telegram from the hospital.

MATTIE: (*Lowering her gun*) How do you know it's for me? What makes you think I am who you think I am?

BLYTHE: The sign on the fence back there ...

MATTIE: The sign says FOR SALE ...

BLYTHE: The other one ... Aren't you Mattie Trueridge?

MATTIE: It depends ...

BLYTHE: I was told it was important.

MATTIE: (*Shrugs*) Come up here on the porch and tell me what this is all about ... My sniffer's good, but I don't hear all that well. (BLYTHE *reluctantly steps up onto the porch.*)

BLYTHE: (*Loudly*) Are you Mattie Trueridge?

MATTIE: I heard that part all ready, thank you ... Now you just sit down, honey-chile and take a load off your feet ... It's a nice warm night, isn't it? Smell that honeysuckle. It cheers you right up.

BLYTHE: I have work to do ... It's a matter of life and death.

MATTIE: Everything is in this world ... Everything is ... I'm surprised the hounds didn't chase you. Charlie chases everything that moves.

BLYTHE: One of them chased me ...

MATTIE: That's Charlie ...

BLYTHE: As long as I was on my bike, he kept nipping at my heels, but as soon as I stopped, he seemed friendly enough. I had to walk the last quarter of the mile ...

MATTIE: Help yourself to some molasses.

BLYTHE: Molasses?

MATTIE: Get your strength back ... That's one of the reasons I still have my own teeth ... (*Shows her teeth*) Not many people my age still have their own teeth ... My first husband used to hold his teeth in his hand, and when he'd leave in the morning he'd say "I'm going outside to bite a hunk out of the world."

BLYTHE: (*Squirming*) Are you sure you're Mattie Trueridge? I don't want to deliver the telegram to the wrong person.

MATTIE: Stop your fidgeting ... Do you have to go to the toilet?

BLYTHE: No, ma'am.

MATTIE: It's out back ...

BLYTHE: I don't have to go ... honest ... I'm not used to sitting still, unless I'm on my bicycle.

MATTIE: Who do you think I am? Lady Godiva? ... Who else would live out this way but me? That's the reason I

SCENE THREE

can't get nobody to buy this place. It's too far out. I can't even get poor white trash interested. I might as well be selling ice to the Eskimos. (BLYTHE *extends the telegram.*)

BLYTHE: Don't you want your telegram?

MATTIE: No siree bob.

BLYTHE: But it's from the hospital ... with news about your son.

MATTIE: How do you know what it's about? Do you go around reading other people's messages? ... That's the trouble with this world. Nothing's private anymore. In the first house I was in, we used to have a phone in the kitchen and every time I'd pick it up, the party line would be right there listening in. I wouldn't be surprised if everybody in the whole world knows what Mattie Trueridge does out here, sitting on the front porch with her dogs, getting drunk on molasses ... Can't get drunk on molasses. That's the hell of it.

BLYTHE: I didn't read the message ... honest ... I don't know what's in it ... I just rode all the way out to bring it to you ... five miles out, five miles back. That's a long way ...

MATTIE: Are you trying to hit me up for money, missey? It won't do you any good cause I ain't got none. The Trueridges got wiped out in the Depression like everybody else ... Not that we had no stock of course.

BLYTHE: I just meant that it's a long way for me to come if you don't take the message. (*Removes a pad from her jacket pocket.*) You see you have to sign for it, so Mr. Hall has proof you got it.

MATTIE: Who's this Mr. Hall that he's got to have proof from me?

BLYTHE: He's my boss. You see the last boy he hired used to go out and get drunk and throw the telegrams in a ditch ... That's why Mr. Hall hired me. But I've got to give him proof that I did my job. (MATTIE *spits a wad of tobacco against the porch railing.*)

MATTIE: Don't talk to me about bosses. I don't have no proof that I done my work, do I?

BLYTHE: Could you just sign it?

MATTIE: I don't sign nothing.

BLYTHE: Why not?

MATTIE: Because I can't write, that's why ... And what's more, I don't want to write ... So what do you think about that, Miss Western Union?

BLYTHE: If you'll just make an X, I'll print your name in.

MATTIE: Maybe ... Maybe not ... I'm thinking about it. And when I think, I do some mighty tall thinking.

BLYTHE: Do you want me to open it for you?

MATTIE: I'll open my own mail, if you please. (BLYTHE *tries to place the telegram in* MATTIE'S *palm.*)

BLYTHE: Here ...

MATTIE: No. I don't take bad news from strangers. It's hard enough to take it from people you know.

BLYTHE: It might not be bad news.

MATTIE: I've never seen a telegram bring good news yet ... Especially at night ... (*An owl hoots*) Shut up, you mangy old owl.

BLYTHE: I can read it to you.

MATTIE: I can read it myself when the time comes. Just because I can't write, it doesn't mean that I can't read. Reading's one thing, and writing's another ... Now you just put that telegram down on the swing between us, and don't you touch it, don't you leave a finger on it, you just leave it right there, because old Mattie knows what it says. After all I wasn't born yesterday.

BLYTHE: (*Hesitating*) Is your son badly sick?

MATTIE: You hush now. You don't say anything like that. You don't speak bad things aloud. Now if you want to talk

Scene Three

to Mattie, you talk about the good things, you talk about the moon or the smell of honeysuckle, but don't say nothing about my boy being sick because no good can come of that, no good at all ... The last time I got a telegram was when my husband was in the war, and I didn't like that one either ...

BLYTHE: Maybe your son's all right. I mean, you really don't know until you open the envelope.

MATTIE: I know ... I know my Matthew ... As long as I don't open that envelope, he's exactly the way he was when I last seen him ... not one whit better, not one whit worse, just holding his own like he used to, like he used to hold his own against the pump down there ... Of course, you don't know my Matthew, do you?

BLYTHE: No, ma'am ...

MATTIE: Of course you wouldn't, being white, but all I got to do is sit on this here swing and close my eyes and I can see him down at the pump, a little tyke of a thing, not much bigger than the pump itself, and he's tugging on it with all his might, pulling down with his body, trying to take his Daddy's place ... I mean he must not be more than six or seven and he's lugging those big pails of water ... and I mean big pails ... into the kitchen (BLYTHE *locates a handkerchief in her uniform pocket and blows her nose.*) What's the matter, honey ... got a cold?

BLYTHE: It's chilly out here, that's all ...

MATTIE: Well you got what you deserve. I don't know what's got into your head for you to come pedalling all the way out here just to bring me bad news. I was just sitting out here, minding my own business, listening to the owls ...

BLYTHE: I thought you'd might like to know.

MATTIE: I don't want to know. Do you understand me?

BLYTHE: Yes, ma'am.

MATTIE: You tell me what I born my children for? Can you tell me that? ... If you can't, then why do you ride around, trespassing on other people's lives?

BLYTHE: I better be going, ma'am.

MATTIE: Yes, maybe you better before I sic Charlie on you ...

BLYTHE: Are you sure you don't want to sign for it? I mean so I can show it to Mr. Hall? (MATTIE *grabs* BLYTHE *by the shoulders and holds her steady, staring fiercely into her eyes.*)

MATTIE: Honey, I'm sorry to lose my temper on you. My son's all right ... You understand that, don't you? (BLYTHE *nods weakly.*) Now you just go as fast as you can, you pedal out here faster than the wind because nobody wants to see a light face out this way this time of night ...

BLYTHE: I didn't mean to bring you any bad news ... It's not my fault. (BLYTHE *runs off the porch into the darkness, leaving the porch swing swinging back and forth* ... MATTIE *snatches up the telegram that lies on the swing.*)

MATTIE: And you be careful of those hounds ... Except for Charlie because he's all right ... If they start nipping at your heels, you just kick them a good one in the nose ... hard ... 'cause the nose is the most sensitive spot. (MATTIE *holds the telegram close to her face and smells it, then without opening it, she neatly folds it and places it into the pocket of her dress. She sits back down in the swing and opens the barrel of the shot-gun, placing it across her lap. There is the sound of a dog or two chasing a bicycle rider into the distance.*)

(*Lights out*)

Scene Four

(*We are back in the Western Union office with* WINTHROP HALL *sitting at the telegraph key, clicking a message across the wires. He is in his shirtsleeves, and wears a green shade over his eyes.*)

(*The clock on the wall, with its official Western Union time, reads 8:30. A radio plays some big-band music.*)

WINTHROP: (*Muttering to himself*) 8:30 at night and I'm still hunched over the telegraph while the swells are out dancing

SCENE FOUR   17

and the wise guys coming in here higgledy-piggedly, each and every mother's son of them wants to send WAR AND PEACE over the wires for ten cents. Nothing's cheap enough for them bums anymore ... except me. I can be put on the old slave box and auctioned off to any high hat waving a fin ... It doesn't make sense. I could have won the lottery just as easily as the next guy. (BLYTHE *enters*)

BLYTHE: Hi, Mr. Hall. Did you think I got lost?

WINTHROP: (*Relieved, but not going to let it show*) What took you so long? ... I thought you might have taken a vacation to Florida with all the other suckers. You know the world don't stop just because you want to go galavanting around nigger town. (*He hands her his half-finished bottle of Moxie.*) Here, finish this bottle of Moxie for me ... I wouldn't even buy it if you didn't like the stuff so much.

BLYTHE: Thanks.

WINTHROP: Rot your teeth out. (BLYTHE *reaches into the basket of messages.*) Leave those messages alone ... it's getting too late for you to go out again. I'll have Rudy take them when he gets back ... (*He selects one*) You can drop this last one off at the hotel on your way home ... Some bastard over there won the Irish Sweepstakes. He ought to give you one big tip. (BLYTHE, *placing the telegram into her jacket pocket, slumps onto the long bench used by the customers.*)

BLYTHE: That's good. I'm getting tired of delivering bad news all the time.

WINTHROP: (*Gently teasing her*) You are, are you, Miss Hifaluting Britches ... You're hardly on the job three weeks, and I suppose you're thinking of joining the Commie strikers, are ye? If you remember correctly, Mrs. Astor, I didn't exactly twist your arm to take this job ... No siree, Mrs. Vanderbilt, I didn't get down on my knees and beg you ... (*During the above,* WINTHROP *has taken* BLYTHE'S *receipt book and has been idly flipping through it.*) I don't see the receipt here from Mrs. Trueridge.

BLYTHE: She didn't want to sign the receipt.

WINTHROP: What do you mean she didn't want to sign the receipt?

BLYTHE: I showed her the book. I explained everything to her. I offered to write her name in for her ...

WINTHROP: Don't you go writing in other people's names.

BLYTHE: Well I didn't. But you can't say I didn't try.

WINTHROP: Then what did you leave the telegram for? No tickee, no laundry.

BLYTHE: What difference does it make? The telegram's paid for, isn't it?

WINTHROP: And suppose the senders claim that Mrs. Trueridge never got the telegram, what do we have for proof? ... I can't afford to send all the way out there again. I didn't want you to have to go all the way out there in the first place.

BLYTHE: She got the telegram ... I didn't throw it into a ditch.

WINTHROP: Now, don't get on your high horse ... I not accusing you of anything, I believe you ...

BLYTHE: (*Wanting to change the subject*) You know I'm beginning to get tired of Moxie ... Why don't you have Miss Hollandish send something else over?

WINTHROP: Pardon me, your highness. Next I'll send out for champagne ... (*Handing her back the receipt book*) How can anybody refuse to sign a receipt?

BLYTHE: Don't ask me how, but she didn't. She didn't even read the telegram ... Maybe she didn't want to sign when she didn't know what she was getting.

WINTHROP: (*Putting on his jacket*) She better read it soon. She has to make funeral arrangements for her son.

BLYTHE: He's dead then?

WINTHROP: Of course, he's dead. Would I send you all the way out there if it weren't important? ... I'm stepping out for a few minutes, so hold down the fort.

BLYTHE: Going to see Miss Hollandish?

SCENE FOUR

WINTHROP: This is no time to be jealous ... (BLYTHE *reddens slightly.* WINTHROP *returning*) I almost forgot. Some guy was in here looking for you earlier ... A tall thin man, about forty years old brown hair, unshaven ... He wouldn't leave his name, but he said he'd be back. (BLYTHE *gives a start*) He didn't say when.

BLYTHE: How did he know I was here?

WINTHROP: You think it's your old man?

BLYTHE: I don't have an old man. (*In a friendly gesture,* WINTHROP *ruffles* BLYTHE'S *hair.*)

WINTHROP: Don't worry, kid. If you don't want him hanging around here, I'll take care of it.

BLYTHE: I can take care of myself.

WINTHROP: I'm sure you can. Just don't bite off anybody's head while I'm gone.

(WINTHROP *exits. As soon as* BLYTHE *is certain that he has really left, she crosses to his desk and opens the folder where the duplicates of telegrams are kept before they are filed. She locates the one to* MRS. TRUERIDGE, *reads it quickly to herself, and biting her lower lip, she sits down in* MR. HALL'S *chair. As she sits, a huge shadow falls across the desk. She looks up and there standing in the doorway is her father,* ALBERT POL DONNER, *whose appearance fits closely the description as given by* BLYTHE'S *boss, with the addition that* AL *is wearing a long, dirty, navy-blue coat with a blue stocking cap on his head, something of a Merchant Marine outfit. He takes a thoughtful puff from his cigarette.*)

AL: (*He's been drinking*) Hiya Pumpkin, I bet you thought you'd never see me again. (BLYTHE *doesn't move*) Don't tell me you don't have a kiss for you old man. (*Silence*) You think I'm a ghost?

BLYTHE: I'm busy right now ... Can't you see that I'm busy? (*She tries to pass him, trying to reach the door.* AL *grabs her wrist.*)

AL: Hey, is this any way to greet me?

BLYTHE: I've got to close the door.

AL: (*Holding her*) Look at me. I rode the rails to get back to you ... with the dicks after me, wanting to bust my head in at every lousy water stop.

BLYTHE: Too bad they didn't ... (*He slaps her, then realizing what he has done, holds onto her with regret.*)

AL: Hey, Pumpkin, I didn't mean that, honest ... I mean you shouldn't provoke me like that ... It's just a love tap right? ... I didn't hurt you, right? ... Say something, will you?

BLYTHE: You didn't hurt me ...

AL: (*Releasing his grip*) You know I love you, honey ... It's the only thing that kept me going ... You got me upset ... I'm tired ... I haven't slept in over thirty-six hours ...

BLYTHE: How did you know I was here?

AL: The druggist up the street told me ...

BLYTHE: (*Matter of factly*) You don't smell so good ...

AL: The beer?

BLYTHE: The coat ...

AL: Yeah ... Well I know ... But it's been through a lot ... Did you think maybe I'd come back in a tuxedo with money dripping from my pockets?

BLYTHE: I didn't think anything ... I didn't think you'd come back at all.

AL: (*Trembling*) How's Momma? ... She feeling any better?

BLYTHE: Do you care?

AL: Pumpkin, don't be so hard on me, huh?

BLYTHE: Don't call me Pumpkin! Why is it so hard for everybody to remember that I have a name?

AL: I know you have a right to be angry ... (*Helplessly*) I thought about walking over to the house, but I don't know if I should ... Not if she's not feeling well ... Maybe it

Scene Four   21

wouldn't be good for her? I thought that perhaps when you got done with work we could ...

BLYTHE: (*Retreating behind* MR. HALL'S *desk*) What happened to your floozy?

AL: Floozy? Who told you that? What has Liz been telling you?

BLYTHE: It must have been cozy, both of you riding the rails, what with that coat of yours ...

AL: Blythe, don't talk about things you don't understand ...

BLYTHE: I think you had better leave before Mr. Hall gets back ...

AL: Blythe, I've come to get you ...

BLYTHE: I don't want to be got ... Why are you limping?

AL: When I jumped from the train, I banged my leg against a log ... Maybe I better sit down ... (AL *starts toward the chair by* MR. HALL'S *desk, but before he reaches it the door to the office opens and a tall man in a chauffeur's uniform enters. His livery is complete, down to white gloves. He is the chauffeur to* MRS. R.F. MILLINGTON, *leading socialite and granddaughter of the town's founding father.*)

CHAUFFEUR: (*Clears throat*) Excuse me, but are you still open for business?

AL: No.

BLYTHE: Yes.

CHAUFFEUR: Mrs. Millington is waiting outside in her limousine, and she wishes to have a message sent to Chicago ... (*Turns toward* ALBERT DONNER) Are you the manager here?

BLYTHE: No. I am. (CHAUFFEUR *glances toward* MR. DONNER *for confirmation.*)

CHAUFFEUR: Really?

AL: Really.

BLYTHE: Mr. Hall is out, but I'm holding down the fort ... (*To her father*) Is there anything else I can do for you, sir?

AL: Will you take a message to your mother?

BLYTHE: Do you wish to send a telegram or should I call the police? We don't allow loitering around here. (AL *puts his cap back on.*)

AL: O.K. Blythe, I can see you're busy ... But I'll be back for you ...

BLYTHE: I won't be here.

CHAUFFEUR: (*Confused*) Are you sure that this is the right place?

BLYTHE: Do you want to send a telegram? (*From his inside coat pocket, the* CHAUFFEUR *removes a scented pink envelope and opens it, removing the note inside.*)

CHAUFFEUR: Perhaps I had better wait for the person in charge.

BLYTHE: I'll see that the message gets sent ... Let me just print it on this yellow pad ...

CHAUFFEUR: Mrs. Millington and her sister raise Siamese cats, and her sister's cat has just given birth, so she wants to send a telegram ... You see, that's the sister's address on top ...

BLYTHE: Let me just copy it down ... It's 75 cents for the first ten words, and then a nickel per word thereafter ...

CHAUFFEUR: (*Reading the message*) Dear Tamara ... Many congratulations on your blessed event. May you produce many more champions ... Love and sardines from Fran Millington ... Do the names count?

BLYTHE: Everything counts after the address ... Now this is to be delivered to the cat?

CHAUFFEUR: (*Almost apologetically*) That's what Mrs. Millington instructed ...

BLYTHE: That will be a dollar and a quarter ...

SCENE FOUR

CHAUFFEUR: You don't mind if I bother you for a receipt?

BLYTHE: No bother at all. (CHAUFFEUR *replaces his cap.*)

CHAUFFEUR: I suppose it sounds strange ... But I guess these are very strange times we're living in. (BLYTHE *hands him the receipt.*)

(Lights out)

(End of Act One)

ACT TWO

Scene One

(*The Western Union sign has been replaced by a sign that reads* HOTEL BALLANGER. *The sign blinks on and off for a few moments through the darkness, and then the lights come up on the desk of* MARK BALLANGER, *the manager and son of the Hotel's owner. He stands at his desk, quietly reading a newspaper, but as soon as the lights are up to full he looks directly at the audience and speaks.*)

MANAGER: And so times are getting so bad that when a person checks into the hotel, I say what do you want the room for—for sleeping or for jumping out of? I figure that if it's only for jumping out of that I shouldn't charge the whole rate, not if they don't mess up the sheets or anything ... Of course, some of them, I suppose, don't take the joke so well ... (*He turns to the radio and listens for a few seconds.*) Kate Smith ... I wouldn't want to miss her for all the tea in China. Of course, that's what I say. Wouldn't it be funny if there weren't any tea in China? I wouldn't put it past them. You don't know who to trust any more.

(*Lights out on the hotel manager. The music from the Kate Smith show segues to music coming from a radio in one of the hotel rooms. The lights come up on a small, shabby room with its window open and yellow curtains blowing gently, blown in part by a small electric fan sitting on the nightstand by the rumpled bed. Next to the bed is an overstuffed chair covered with heavy fabric with floral patterns. No one is in the room. At last,* MRS. HORACE DESMOND, *in a pink slip and bra, emerges from the bathroom carrying a glass and a bottle of homemade gin.*)

MRS. DESMOND: (*Looks at alarm clock*) Goddamn you, Leslie, how long are you going to stay out? (*There's a knock at the door.*)

MRS. DESMOND: Who's there?

Scene One

BLYTHE: Western Union.

MRS. DESMOND: Christ ... Are you sure?

BLYTHE: Yes, ma'am.

MRS. DESMOND: Just a minute. (*She locates a robe and slippers. After a few adjustments, she opens the door.*) Come in. (*As if almost afraid of being seen by somebody in the hallway she almost pulls* BLYTHE *inside and closes the door after her.* BLYTHE *glances about curiously, almost forgetting what she's there for.* MRS. DESMOND *whistles.*) You got telegram for me, kid?

BLYTHE: It's for a Mr. Leslie Greeley.

MRS. DESMOND: (*Crossing to the bed where her pocketbook is.*) Yeah, well, I knew it couldn't be for me. Nobody knows I'm here ... But I'm his ... wife, so you can leave it here.

BLYTHE: You have to sign the receipt.

MRS. DESMOND: That's all right, I'm just trying to locate some change for a tip.

BLYTHE: (*Hoping to inspire generosity*) I think your husband won the Irish Sweepstakes.

MRS. DESMOND: What? ... Say that again, kid slowly.

BLYTHE: I think your husband won the Irish Sweepstakes.

MRS. DESMOND: Where is it? Let me see it ... Let me see it ... (BLYTHE *fumbles into her pocket and removes yellow messages.*)

BLYTHE: That's what my boss said when he took the message.

MRS. DESMOND: (*Reading quickly*) Is this some kind of joke?

BLYTHE: No. He really won.

MRS. DESMOND: But this telegram says, "Dear Tamara, many congratulations on your blessed event. May you produce many more champions ... Love and Sardines from Fran Millington ..."

BLYTHE: Oh, I'm sorry, you took the wrong message ... That's a practice one ... I was practising sending telegrams before I came over ... You can tell it's not yours ... See, this is yours ... (*Hands her the other message.*)

MRS. DESMOND: Love and sardines? What kind of a crackpot outfit is Western Union running?

BLYTHE: It's to a cat ... I was taking a copy home to show my mother.

MRS. DESMOND: Shit on the cat ... Let me see how much money he's won ... (*Reads quickly*) Dear Mr. Greeley, this is to notify you that your number, 567-8764-856, has been selected as the grand-prize winner in this year's Irish Sweepstakes. $28,000 awaits you on presentation of your ticket ... Oh my god, oh my god, oh my god ... (*She falls back on the bed in a daze of happiness, rereading the telegram.*) Dear Mr. Greeley, this is to notify you that your number, 567-8764-856, has been selected as the grand-prize winner in this year's Irish Sweepstakes ... $28,000 awaits you ... Did you ever hear any sweeter words in your entire life? ... Did you? Did you? ... $28,000 awaits you on presentation of your ticket ... pinch me, pinch me, pinch me ... I can't be dreaming, can I? Tell me you're real, honey ... You're real, aren't you?

BLYTHE: I think so.

MRS. DESMOND: Oh, when Leslie sees this he's going right through the ceiling, there'll be dancing on the rooftops ... Oh, honey, when he left here he was so depressed, you just don't know ... But now everything has been made right, as if by magic ... I'll tell you what you are, honey, you're magic ... Western Union is magic ... You're coming in here, bringing news like this ...

BLYTHE: (*Bluffing for a tip*) Maybe I should be going, ma'am ...

MRS. DESMOND: Oh no, you've got to wait for Leslie's return ... You've got to see the expression on his face ... I mean you're going to get such a big tip ... For chrissakes, honey, I can't give you fifty cents for news like this ... He's going to be back soon, just you wait ... Please ... I don't know what I'm doing, you've got to sit here and celebrate with me ... Let me pour a drink for you ... Oh you don't

SCENE ONE

know what this means to us ... 28,000 marvelous dollars ... I'll have George Washington's face all over the place.

BLYTHE: I'm sorry, but I don't drink, ma'am.

MRS. DESMOND: Of course you drink ... Everybody drinks ... Even Mrs. Fishface's cats drink ...

BLYTHE: Mrs. Millington ...

MRS. DESMOND: Whoever it was ...

BLYTHE: Could you just sign the receipt? ... I have to have a receipt for my boss.

MRS. DESMOND: Work for a real grouch-puss, huh?

BLYTHE: Nah, he's all right.

MRS. DESMOND: For $28,000 I'll write you a book ... (*Scribbles her name*) How many receipts do you want ... I'll give you all the receipts you want ... Hold it. I think there's some glasses in the bathroom ... Don't go away, because I don't want to celebrate alone ... I hate to be happy alone ... It's so wasteful ... (*As she crosses toward the window, she leans out shouting.*) Leslie, will you hurry up home? Have I got news for you ... That should shock them in this one-horse town ... (*Returns from the bathroom*) My boobs hanging out the window ... (*Jumps up on the bed, dancing, clinking the glasses together*) Read me that telegram again, honey ...

BLYTHE: The one about the cats?

MRS. DESMOND: No ... Leslie's ... Read me that ... Nobody has ever written anything so beautiful in my whole life ... That's literature ... You have been selected as grand-prize winner ...

BLYTHE: Can I ask you a question?

MRS. DESMOND: (*Pouring*) You're going to have some gin, right? ... Of course you are ... only the world's greatest grouch-puss wouldn't celebrate with me tonight ...

BLYTHE: But you signed the receipt Ada Desmond ...

MRS. DESMOND: I did?

BLYTHE: Aren't you Mrs. Greeley?

MRS. DESMOND: Of course I'm Mrs. Greeley ... What kind of a woman do you think I am? ... I just signed it with my maiden name, that's all ... that's what it is ... I just signed it with my maiden name.

BLYTHE: Well then could you perhaps write your married name in so that Mr. Hall won't think I gave it to the wrong person?

MRS. DESMOND: Sure, honey ... We don't want your Mr. Hall thinking that, do we? ... We certainly don't want Mr. Hall thinking that ... Here, let's raise our glasses to a toast ... a toast to Mr. Hall and his shitload of receipts ... Excuse me, honey, I didn't mean to talk like that ...

BLYTHE: That's o.k. My friend Reedy Miller talks like a sailor ... (BLYTHE *tastes her gin and makes a face.*)

MRS. DESMOND: What's the matter, honey, don't you like the taste of it?

BLYTHE: It doesn't taste like Moxie ...

MRS. DESMOND: Christ, nothing does ... Nothing tastes the same anymore ... (*Falls back on the bed, laughing sadly.*) Look, kid, what's your name?

BLYTHE: Blythe ... Blythe Donner, the last name is like the ...

MRS. DESMOND: (*Interrupting*) Well, Blythe, I can trust you, can't I? ... Of course I can ... If I can't trust a trusted servant of Western Union who can I trust ... (*Starts to say something, then changes her mind.*) Look, I'll tell you what, Blythe ... When Leslie gets back, I'm going to make him give you a hundred-dollar tip ... You'd like that, wouldn't you? The promise of a hundred dollars?

BLYTHE: I'd like that a lot.

MRS. DESMOND: (*Laughing*) Of course you would. Who wouldn't like a hundred dollars ... I could use a hundred-dollar tip myself ... (*Raising her glass*) Ladies and

Gentleworms, what this country needs is a good five cent, one-hundred dollar tip ... Honey, just drink up. You'll get used to the taste of it.

BLYTHE: Yes, ma'am.

MRS. DESMOND: And don't call me ma'am. Call me Ada ... Ma'am makes me feel a hundred years old and I'm only ... God, I'm only ninety ... You know, I had my first drink when I was fifteen years old ... A high school boy named Johnny Brewster wanted to get me drunk so he could ... you can imagine what he wanted ... but did I fool him ... All I did was get sick and throw up all over him ... That discouraged his romantic intentions.

BLYTHE: Maybe I shouldn't drink so much ...

MRS. DESMOND: This is better than the stuff he was giving me, I can tell you that ... Moonshine right from his father's still ... I asked you before ... Can I trust you?

BLYTHE: I don't know ...

MRS. DESMOND: Of course I can ... What difference does it make? Right? Right ... Twenty-eight thousand dollars! Who would have thought that you'd come walking through the door with twenty-eight thousand dollars ... Let me tell you something, honey ... I don't want to lie to you ... I don't want to lie to anybody ... I'm not really Leslie's wife ... at least not officially ... But what difference does that make, right? Because now Leslie and I can afford to get married ... Before, we couldn't even afford to pay for my divorce because Leslie had all these stocks and the bottom just dropped out of the goddamn market ... excuse my French ... But now we can afford a few things ... That's why I can say that I'm his wife and not be ashamed of anything ... not of anything, you understand?

BLYTHE: I think so ...

MRS. DESMOND: Are you married? Of course you're not married. You're not even old enough to drink ... Blythe, if you only knew the sonuvabitch I'm married to ... so tight, he squeaks when he walks. He doesn't care where I am, who

I'm with ... He deserves everything that happens to him ... Let me tell you, honey, that as soon as Leslie cashes that lovely check of his I'm going over and kick dust in Harry's face. You think they've seen dust in Oklahoma? They haven't seen a speck of dust until they see the dust I'm going to kick in my husband's face ... So tight you'd have to oil his pockets to slide a nickel out ... (*She laughs*) Don't you think that's funny, kid?

BLYTHE: (*Trying*) I think so ...

MRS. DESMOND: Then if it's funny, laugh ... I want to hear a lot of laughter in this room ... I want this crummy room filled with laughter ... It's been so gloomy around here lately that you could cut it with a knife ... that's what you could do with it ... cut it with a knife and serve it with baloney sandwiches.

BLYTHE: You think he's going to be back soon?

MRS. DESMOND: Any minute, baby, any minute ...

BLYTHE: (*Torn between staying and leaving*) Maybe I could just leave you my address and he could just mail ...

MRS. DESMOND: Stay, honey ... Please ... Pretty please ... I want to celebrate in this half-horse town ... You know, Blythe, someday you're going to come into money of your own ... I feel it in my bones ... You're going to come into a pot of money and you're going to know what this feeling is ...

BLYTHE: What's it feel like?

MRS. DESMOND: It's better than getting drunk ... that's what it is ... better than drunk. (BLYTHE *opens her mouth wide and holds out her tongue for inspection.*)

BLYTHE: Do you think I'm getting drunk?

MRS. DESMOND: (*Drifting*) Someday you're going to be so rich ... I can imagine you having breakfast in bed ... Lobster in bed ...

BLYTHE: I don't think I'd like lobster ...

Scene One

MRS. DESMOND: Doughnuts then, with servants waiting on you hand and foot ... And that Mr. Hall will call you up on the phone ... You'll have a private phone of course ...

BLYTHE: (*Aristocratically*) Of course ...

MRS. DESMOND: And he'll beg you to deliver telegrams for him ... He'll get down on his knees and beg, and you'll tell him, in a voice choking with diamonds as big as the Ritz, "Oh I'm sorry, Mr. Hall, but I have a date with the Duke and Duchess Greeley to go on a fox-hunt through Astor Country. I'm afraid that you'll just have to close down that little old Western Union of yours. That's all there is to it." ... No more telegrams. Wouldn't that be heaven? No more shitty messages ... Just lottery tickets ... Winning lottery tickets for everybody.

BLYTHE: I have a feeling I'll never be that rich.

(*There's a knock at the door.*)

MRS. DESMOND: Of course you will ... the communists will make everybody rich ... Why sure they will, honey ... That's the direction this country of ours is going ... After all, a depression don't last forever ... Nothing lasts forever.

BLYTHE: (*Hopeful*) I think someone's at the door.

MRS. DESMOND: Leslie, is that you ... Guess what ...

MANAGER: Mrs. Greeley?

MRS. DESMOND: (*Panicked*) Who is it?

MANAGER: Mark Ballanger ... The manager ...

MRS. DESMOND: Christ ... What does he want? ... We paid in advance ... (*Takes the glass from* BLYTHE *and hides the glasses and the gin under the bed.*) Just a moment ... (*To* BLYTHE) I don't want him to think I'm corrupting a minor. (*She adjusts her robe and hair.*) I'm coming ... (*She crosses to the door and opens it. Standing in the hallway is the hotel manager and a uniformed policeman.*)

MRS. DESMOND: The police?

HOTEL MANAGER: Mrs. Greeley?

MRS. DESMOND: Yes ...

HOTEL MANAGER: Don't be alarmed.

MRS. DESMOND: What's this all about?

HOTEL MANAGER: (*Quietly*) This is Officer Milton. Would it be all right if we came in for a few minutes?

MRS. DESMOND: (*Confused*) No ...

HOTEL MANAGER: I'm afraid it's about your husband.

MRS. DESMOND: Horace? ... Is Horace all ...

OFFICER MILTON: Aren't you Mrs. Leslie Greeley?

MRS. DESMOND: Of course.

OFFICER MILTON: Then I'm afraid we have some bad news for you, ma'am.

MRS. DESMOND: Bad news?

OFFICER MILTON: About a half hour ago, your husband was found under one of the piers ...

MRS. DESMOND: What?

OFFICER MILTON: (*Sympathetically*) Perhaps you'd better sit down, Mrs. Greeley. (BLYTHE *leaps up and gives her chair to* MRS. DESMOND, *helping her.*)

MRS. DESMOND: What do you mean? Is he all right? Is Leslie all right?

OFFICER MILTON: There's a bullet hole through his head, ma'am ...

MANAGER: What are you still doing here?

BLYTHE: I was just waiting ...

MRS. DESMOND: (*Overlapping*) Somebody shot Leslie?

OFFICER MILTON: Suicide, ma'am ... We believe it's sucide. The gun was found in his hand.

Scene One

MRS. DESMOND: (*The news beginning to sink.*) No, that's impossible ... impossible ... are you sure?

OFFICER MILTON: There was a wallet on him ... Of course we'd like you to come down to the station to make a positive identification ... Whenever you feel up to it ...

MRS. DESMOND: (*Anguished*) Ain't that a crock ...

OFFICER MILTON: (*Recognizing* BLYTHE'S *presence*) Who's this? You a relative?

BLYTHE: I'm from Western Union ...

HOTEL MANAGER: (*To* OFFICER) Mrs. Donner's daughter .. Blythe, maybe you had better run along home ... (MRS. DESMOND *grasping desperately for comfort.*)

MRS. DESMOND: No ... Please, honey ... Don't leave ...

BLYTHE: (*Not knowing how to react*) Ada ... (MRS. DESMOND *holds her.*)

MRS. DESMOND: I don't want to be alone ... This is all a bad dream ...

OFFICER MILTON: (*Genuinely sorry*) We're awfully sorry, Ma'am ...

HOTEL MANAGER: (*Awkwardly*) If there's anything we can ... please feel free ... (*His voice trails off.*)

MRS. DESMOND: (*Sobbing*) No ... You don't understand ... None of you understand ...

HOTEL MANAGER: Would you like me to call the doctor ...

BLYTHE: I've got my bicycle outside ... Ada, let me go get Doctor Wilson ...

MRS. DESMOND: (*Hysterically*) Oh God oh God oh God ...

OFFICER MILTON: (*To the* MANAGER) You'd better call the Doc ...

HOTEL MANAGER: (*Exiting*) I'll call him ...

OFFICER MILTON: Do you have anything to drink, ma'am?

BLYTHE: She has something under the bed ...

MRS. DESMOND: (*To* BLYTHE) Oh honey, honey, honey ...

OFFICER MILTON: (*Getting the gin*) Maybe she ought to lie down.

BLYTHE: Ada, let me help you up ...

MRS. DESMOND: Oh if you only knew ... If you only knew ... If you only knew ... If anybody only knew ... (OFFICER MILTON *stands helplessly and pours a stiff helping of gin into the glass while* MRS. DESMOND *clutches* BLYTHE *to her.*) What did I do to deserve this, Blythe ... What did I do?

(*Lights out*)

Scene Two

(*Dream sequence No. 2*)

(*We are now at the outer reaches of space, on the planet Tamara. A creature in a space-suit floats through the artificial atmosphere, destroying the manticore-triumphants—fantastic cat-like creatures who lurk under the steel piers used for launching rockets.* CHESS SHIRE'S *Buck Rogers disintegrating ray gun blazes through the darkness, its laser beams caressing the sardinic-triumphants with destruction.* CHESS'S *robot partner, XT-N-R4, enters, walking with weighted space suit and boots, and carrying a space helmet. Its mechanical fingers clutch a bunch of tyconderogas or moon-strokes, bizarre artificial flowers, along with a printout of his tricentennial mother's day poem. Computerlike blips punctuate the silence.*)

CHESS SHIRE: (*Astronaut*) Hey, XT-N-R4, did you see the way I zapped the nose off that Siamese Sardinic-Triumphant? Some shooting, huh? Tamara's answer to Tom Mix —that's what they call me.

XT-N-R4: If you keep zapping them like that, Chess, the Sardinic Triumphants, subspecies Siamese, are going to be extinct in no time.

CHESS: Serves them right. It's the only way to communicate with them. The death ray's the only thing those animals

Scene Two

understand ... (*Noticing the flowers*) What are you doing with those moon-strokes?

XT-N-R4: Since your memory unit is fallible, I take it that you forget that tomorrow, Sub-Trueridge Lunar Month, is the Tricentennial of Mechanical Motherhood.

CHESS: You're a robot. What do you care about Motherhood? It's just another one of those artificial holidays to make us spend our hard-earned work units.

XT-N-R4: That's the trouble with Humanoids. You think Robots are like you. Well, we're different ... We have feelings. If you tinker with us, do we not break down? If you wrench us, do we not fall apart? Are we not warmed and cooled by the same controlled humidity as Humanoids?

CHESS: (*Cutting him off*) All right, all right.

XT-N-R4: Well you better care. Last time you forgot, and our computer mother shut off our power. Remember? You couldn't zap a Sardinic-Triumphant for months. See, I have my message ready (*Reads his telegram*):

> Dear Electronic Mother:
> In the face of metapsychosis,
> It's you I adore,
> Your loving robot,
> XT-N-R4.

So you'd better think of something quick or it's going to be all over.

CHESS: That's easy enough for you to say. You've been programmed for such sentiments. I have to think up my own greetings ... All by myself.

XT-N-R4: Our Envoi-messenger is leaving for Earth in a couple of micro-minutes. She's your only hope.

(*A supersonic meow. A Sardinic-Triumphant, land species, rears its abysmally ugly head in the distance* CHESS *holds up a hand mirror, finds his target, and shooting over his shoulder caresses the creature with instant death.*)

CHESS: How can I think and kill at the same time?

XT-N-R4: If you knew as much as robots, you might realize that those giant cats are mere illusions. Their fur has merely been enlarged by cosmic warp.

CHESS: Why must mothers be so demanding?

(BLYTHE *enters. She is dressed in her same costume. The only change is that her traditional cap has been replaced by a space helmet with the words Western Union blinking on and off.* BLYTHE *pushes her bicycle, although this time her bicycle is slightly enhanced by artificial wings.*)

BLYTHE: (*To* XT-N-R4) Western Union. Tamara division, Milky way, reporting for duty, sir.

CHESS: It's the Robot. I'm the Humanoid. I'm the one who needs help. (*Examines bicycle, adds air to the front tire.*) ... for Chrissakes you'd think our astrolab would give you less primitive equipment to work with.

BLYTHE: Communication is not a high-priority technique, sir.

CHESS: You're telling me. Even envoi messengers are obsolete.

XT-N-R4: You must be the last one.

CHESS: The expeditionary Forces wiped them out ... Even if I come up with a message, you won't be able to get it through.

BLYTHE: I'll get it through. I'm not afraid of Sardinic-Triumphants. All you have to do is kick them in the nose.

XT-N-R4: We have to make do with what we have.

CHESS: Even if she traveled as fast as the speed of light it would take years.

XT-N-R4: Here, the Winston Ticonderogas are to be delivered to my electronic mother, sir ... along with this precoded poem.

BLYTHE: I have to put my Buck Rogers seismic ear-plugs in.

SCENE TWO

XT-N-R4: (*Insulted*) You don't wish to hear my poem?

BLYTHE: It's not that. You see the noise level of earth exceeds 150 decibels. It's quite painful to listen to anything down there ... (*To* CHESS) Do Humanoids wish to be remembered?

CHESS: Sure, but I can't think of anything to say.

BLYTHE: Then you might consider our pre-coded Tricentennial telegram, complete with photoelectric moon-strokes and noneroded chocolates. Everyone's sending them.

XT-N-R4: Not robots ... Besides I haven't touched a noneroded chocolate since I was a radio.

CHESS: But I want to send something straight from the heart.

BLYTHE: I'm certain we have what you want ... (*Reads from precoded message.*) ... "dearest Communal Mechanical Mother of the Tri-Centennial, I hereby award you filial devotion as strictly delineated by the subcommittee for standard piety. Love, etc. ..."

CHESS: It does have a certain charm.

BLYTHE: It costs more if you make up your own.

CHAUFFEUR: I'll take it. Along with a box of noneroded chocolates with the carbon-dioxide centers.

XT-N-R4: It's not what you say. It's how you say it.

CHESS: How much?

BLYTHE: Where does it have to go?

CHAUFFEUR: Communal Mechanical Mother Division, Cal Tech, Mid-west Section, Chicago.

BLYTHE: (*Checking rates*) From Tamara to the Earth, it's a dollar thirty-five, from Earth-Station to Chicago is $7,890,678, tax included.

CHESS: Sounds reasonable.

XT-N-R4: The monorails are not what they used to be.

BLYTHE: Will that be cash or charge?

CHESS: (*Removes a single bill.*) Can you change a ten million? (BLYTHE *makes change from a metal coin changer.*)

BLYTHE: I think so.

XT-N-R4: I don't understand why they put Herbert Hoover's picture on that bill.

CHESS: When will you be back?

BLYTHE: By Mercury Solstice at least. (BLYTHE *mounts her bicycle and carries her telegrams off into the region of outer space. In the background an image of Earth spins slowly.*)

XT-N-R4: Look at her ride the light of the stars.

CHESS: I don't know how she got a job like that ... I bet she knows somebody ... It's getting so you've got to have pull to get anywhere in this universe. (*An Apache appears upon the horizon of Tamara. His body is covered with warrior's paint and he gives out a war-whoop. Before he can release his arrows however,* CHESS *turns his Flash Gordon disintegrating ray-gun upon him and caresses him with death.*) I don't know. You give them the best reservations and they still aren't satisfied.

XT-N-R4: (*Bored*) I'm going inside to be watched by television.

CHESS: Wait, I'll go with you.

(*Lights out*)

Scene Three

(*Western Union office. The hands of the official clock read five minutes after midnight. The office is clearly closed, with the green shades drawn on the windows. On stage is* WINTHROP HALL *who is asleep, his head resting on the desk, a half-eaten sandwich resting at his elbow. A small bulb in the desk lamp remains on. A radio at the rear of the office replays a speech by President Franklin Delano Roosevelt—a speech that had been delivered from Washington earlier that afternoon.*)

SCENE THREE 39

VOICE OF ROOSEVELT: "Recently, the most notable public questions that have concerned us all have had to do with industry and labor, and, with respect to these, certain developments have taken place which I consider of importance. I am happy to report that after a year of uncertainty, culminating in the collapse of the spring of 1933, we are bringing order out of the old chaos with a greater certainty of the employment of labor at a reasonable wage and of more business at a fair profit. These governmental and industrial achievements hold promise of new achievements for the nation."

(BLYTHE *enters the main street of the town. She pushes her bicycle and yet she walks slowly and uncertainly, feeling the effects of drinking with* MRS. DESMOND. *A few newspapers and empty paper bags blow through the streets.*)

VOICE OF ROOSEVELT: "Men may differ as to the particular form of governmental activity with respect to industry and business, but nearly all are agreed that private enterprise in times such as these cannot be left without assistance and without reasonable safeguards lest it destroy not only itself but also processes of civilization."

(BLYTHE *parks her bicycle, approaches the door of the office, and unlocks the door. As her key clicks in the lock,* WINTHROP *sits up, startled.*)

VOICE OF ROOSEVELT: "The underlining necessity for such activity is index as strong now as it was years ago where Elihu Root said the following significant words: "Instead of the give-and-take of free individual contract, the tremendous power of organization has combined great aggregations of capital in enormous industrial ..."

(WINTHROP *stands up, stretches, pours some water from his glass onto his hands, and rubs it onto his face.*)

BLYTHE: Mr. Hall, what are doing here?

VOICE OF ROOSEVELT: "... establishments working through vast agencies of commerce and employing great masses of men in movements of production and transportation and trade, so great in the mass that each individual concerned ..."

(WINTHROP, *without acknowledging her presence, crosses to the enormous radio.*)

BLYTHE: (*Closing door*) I didn't think anybody was here.

WINTHROP: (*Switches off radio*) Does your mother know where you are?

BLYTHE: (*Weakly*) She knows ... I called before I left the hotel.

WINTHROP: (*He knows the answer.*) You were at the hotel all this time?

BLYTHE: Yeah ...

WINTHROP: What's the matter, kid? You look a little green around the gills. If you're celebrating St. Patty's day, you're a little late.

BLYTHE: I'm not feeling so well.

WINTHROP: (*Takes her chin*) Blow a little my way, sister.

BLYTHE: (*Gives a sample of her breath.*) I think I'm drunk.

WINTHROP: You don't know?

BLYTHE: It's not my fault.

WINTHROP: (*Releasing her*) Blame it on the economy like everybody else.

BLYTHE: (*False bravado*) I've been drinking with Mrs. Greeley.

WINTHROP: What do you want? A medal? The world is filled with people who drink with Mrs. Greeleys.

BLYTHE: Her husband killed himself.

WINTHROP: So I heard.

BLYTHE: Except it really wasn't her husband.

WINTHROP: I called the hotel to find out what had happened to you because your mother called here. Mark said you were with Greeley's old lady.

BLYTHE: I want to go to the bathroom.

WINTHROP: (*Brings her the pail.*) Here, use this ...

SCENE THREE

BLYTHE: (*Stubborn*) No.

WINTHROP: Use it or I'll give you the back of my hand. You came here to throw up, didn't you?

BLYTHE: I changed my mind.

WINTHROP: You changed your mind ... Tell me that in the morning.

BLYTHE: I didn't have any choice. She needed somebody to drink with.

WINTHROP: I was supposed to take Miss Hollandish to the movies tonight ... To see Flash Gordon ...

BLYTHE. I couldn't get out ...

WINTHROP: I knew I should have gone over and dragged you out ... Are you sure you called your mother?

BLYTHE: I called her ... (BLYTHE *stretches out on the customer's bench.*) She promised me a hundred-dollar tip.

WINTHROP: She did, did she?

BLYTHE: (*Belligerently*) Yes, she did. You ask her yourself.

WINTHROP: When you feel your head tomorrow morning, Lady Astor, you would have earned it.

BLYTHE: Is she going to get the lottery money?

WINTHROP: Not if she's not his wife she ain't.

BLYTHE: That's doesn't seem fair ... She's practically married to him.

WINTHROP: I'm practically the King of England myself.

BLYTHE: She kept filling my glass, and I'd drink some, and then I'd go to the bathroom and pour the rest down the sink ... I'd drink some and I'd sink some ... (*Drifting off*) I'd pour some sink and sink some ...

WINTHROP: Come on, Blythe, you're not going to sleep here. I'm taking you home.

BLYTHE: Don't you wish you could fly through outer space like Flash Gordon?

WINTHROP: Come on, Blythe, upsi-daisy.

BLYTHE: (*Fighting him*) No. I don't want to go home. You can't make me go home if I don't want to.

WINTHROP: What's the matter, kid? You afraid of your mother finding out that you drink like a fish?

BLYTHE: Fish don't drink.

WINTHROP: Don't get technical on me ... I remember the first time I came home plastered. Did the old man take a belt to me and ...

BLYTHE: I can't go home ... My old man ...

WINTHROP: I'm not running a flop house for Gypsy messengers.

BLYTHE: Let me sleep here ... please ... Mr. Hall, I don't want to go home ... I don't ... (WINTHROP *supports* BLYTHE *and opens the front door.*)

WINTHROP: Stop dragging your feet. I know you can walk ... I've seen you walk before.

BLYTHE: No. My old man is out there somewhere.

WINTHROP: So what? There's nothing to be afraid of.

BLYTHE: I'm dizzy ... (BLYTHE *collapses in* WINTHROP'S *arms.*)

WINTHROP: If you're faking kid, so help me ... (WINTHROP *hoists* BLYTHE *to his shoulders and carries her the way he might carry a sack of potatoes. He starts out the door, then returns to get his hat.* BLYTHE'S *father, dressed as before and still under the weather, appears from a side alley.*) You know where I could have been tonight, Miss High-Faluting Britches? I could have been to the movies with Miss Hollandish ... And maybe I could have won a set of dishes ... But not me ... No such luck ... I've got to look out for my employees or the whole lousy semi-socialistic system will come crashing down

Scene Three 43

about my head. (*He thinks better about taking* BLYTHE *home and so he carries her back to the bench.*) All right, Lady Astor, you win. You might as well stay here. You'll be as safe here as you will anywhere else.

(WINTHROP *removes his jacket and places it over his sleeping messenger. By this time* BLYTHE'S *father has entered the office and stands near the opened door. He closes it, not loudly but loud enough.*)

AL: Just what in the hell do you think you're doing?

WINTHROP: (*Startled*) Who's there?

AL: What in the hell do you think you're up to? Keep your hands off my kid.

WINTHROP: Get out of here you bum before I throw you out.

AL: I'm taking Blythe away from here. (WINTHROP *stands between* AL *and his daughter.*)

WINTHROP: (*Forcing* AL *back*) You heard me.

AL: (*Loudly*) What's my daughter doing here? (BLYTHE *groans and stirs uneasily.* WINTHROP *grabs* AL'S *left arm, forces it up behind him, and heards him toward the door.*)

WINTHROP: She's here because she wants to be here. Isn't that good enough for you?

AL: Get your filthy hands off me. (WINTHROP *opens the door and shoves* AL *out onto the street.* AL, *wildly.*) You're molesting my daughter, that's what you're doing. (WINTHROP *slams the door and quickly locks it.* AL *bangs on the door.*) Get you nigger hands off my child ...

WINTHROP: Get away from here before I blow your head off ... (AL *leans pathetically against the door.*)

AL: You're no different than the rest of them ... I've seen you carrying on ... I know what's going on in there ... I wasn't born yesterday ... (WINTHROP *crosses to the office safe, works the combination, opens it, and from a white cloth bag removes a revolver.*) I'm going to have you lynched, you bastard ... You can't keep a white man from his daughter ... It's not right ... You hear me? She's all I got in this world ... Don't you understand? A man has got to have something. (*He has backed down the steps and away from the building, his voice getting louder.*) I'll show you who you are ... I'll show you ... (AL *grabs the lids off garbage pails by the alleyway and bangs the lids together as if they were giant cymbals.*) Everybody wake up ... Get up ... That black bastard in there is raping my daughter ... (WINTHROP, *gun in hand, crosses to the window.* BLYTHE *stirs uneasily, crying out in her sleep.* WINTHROP *raises the window slightly and thrusts the revolver out.*) Do you hear that everybody? That Irish nigger is raping my daughter ...

WINTHROP: For the last time ... I'm warning you ... Go along home ... You don't know what you're saying ...

AL: (*Screams*) Rape!

WINTHROP: I don't want to hear your filthy words anymore ...

VOICE IN THE DISTANCE: "What's going on?", "What's happening?", "Who's out there?", etc.

WINTHROP: You're not fit to clean my boots ...

AL: (*Banging the garbage can lids*) Help me ... Rape ... (WINTHROP *fires.* AL *staggers back, the garbage can lids clattering to the street.* BLYTHE *wakes with a start, sitting up, frightened, gathering garbled, indistinct words.*)

BLYTHE: What? What ... Mr. Hall! ... Mr. Hall! (WINTHROP *crosses slowly to her.*)

WINTHROP: (*Calming her, softly*) Go back to sleep, darling ... It's nothing ... It's only a bad dream.

(End of Act Two)

Act Three

Scene One

(*Railroad station. Sounds of a train disappearing into the distance. Sitting stiffly on one of the benches is* MATTIE TRUERIDGE, *with a small cardboard suitcase by her legs. She sits quietly, holding onto her cane with her left hand, dressed in pretty much the same costume we saw in Act One.*)

(*Farther up the platform stands* MRS. DESMOND, *dressed in an inexpensive black dress, with a black hat and veil. She holds a few wilted flowers. She paces nervously up and down the platform. Back in the main part of the station the clock on the wall, with its official railroad time, says five o'clock. A soldier, with his gear leaning against the machine, plays pinball, and there is the sound of music:* "Brother, Can you Spare a Dime?".)

(*As* MRS. DESMOND *paces past* MATTIE, MATTIE *attempts a conversation.*)

MATTIE: Going far?

MRS. DESMOND: I don't know, mother ... There's no strings on this woman ... I'll get off when I feel like it.

MATTIE: I'm going to Baltimore ... (*No reply*) Maryland ... I have relations in Maryland.

MRS. DESMOND: I've had relations in Maryland myself.

MATTIE: My son is sick in a hospital in Baltimore ... You ever been to Baltimore?

MRS. DESMOND: I just said so, didn't I?

MATTIE: I guess so.

MRS. DESMOND: I've been to Baltimore and to Niagara Falls. The only two places I've been outside of half-horse towns ... That's as far as I have been ... I've been there and back. A few whistle stops in between.

MATTIE: Niagra Falls ... my ... my ... my. That's where folks go on their honeymoon, isn't it?

MRS. DESMOND: Honeymoon? ... Well whatever I went for, I'll tell you something. It doesn't take a week to see water go over a cliff.

MATTIE: I seen a picture of Niagara Falls once ... In one of those things you hold up to your eyes ... I don't know what you call it.

MRS. DESMOND: It's a lot of water all right ... (*Looks at the time*) That's what I like about this country of ours. Even the railroads don't run on time. We're suppose to have all these big brains running things, so what do they do? They collapse the economy on us and then they can't even get us from one place to another.

MATTIE: I rode on a stagecoach once ... But that was a long time ago ... (*No reply*) I don't like to have to ask ... But I wonder if I might ask a favor of you?

MRS. DESMOND: I'm sorry ... I'm not very good at granting favors ... anymore.

MATTIE: I was hoping to find somebody to help me lift my suitcase on the train ...

MRS. DESMOND: I'm sure we can find somebody ... I'll ask the soldier back there if you want ...

MATTIE: That's all right ... I don't want to bother nobody. (POLICE OFFICER MILTON *enters onto the platform.*)

MRS. DESMOND: I'm sure we'll get somebody to help ... This half-horse town ought to be crawling with strong, handsome men willing to do us a favor ... Isn't that right, officer?

OFFICER MILTON: (*Tipping his cap*) That's right, Mrs. Greeley.

MRS. DESMOND: You can call me Ada. There's no need to be formal when a body's leaving town.

OFFICER MILTON: I guess not ... Ada.

Scene One

MRS. DESMOND: Thank you for the flowers ... It was most thoughtful that somebody remembered ...

OFFICER MILTON: I thought I should do something, considering the circumstances ...

MRS. DESMOND: Please, I don't want to talk about it ...

OFFICER MILTON: Sorry ...

MRS. DESMOND: Did you come all the way down to the station just to make certain that I'd make the train?

OFFICER MILTON: Not exactly ...

MRS. DESMOND: Oh?

OFFICER MILTON: I guess you heard about the shooting last night.

MRS. DESMOND: Not me ... I was in no state to listen to anything last night ... And even when I am I'd rather listen to the dance bands than the news. News is only depressing. Somebody's always shooting somebody for some stupid reason, or ex-millionaires throwing themselves out of the window. Ignorance is bliss or don't you know that by now, Officer?

OFFICER MILTON: Milton ... Milton, Milton ... (*Embarrassed*) It was my father's idea.

MRS. DESMOND: Milton Milton ... Oh I've heard worse ... Believe me, much worse.

OFFICER MILTON: (*Wanting to change the subject.*) You haven't seen a big black guy hanging around here this afternoon, have you? Tall, with white hair, with an Irish accent ... He's an Irishman, a black Irishman ... (*To* MATTIE) Have you?

MATTIE: I haven't seen nothing ... I'm just sitting here, looking straight ahead.

OFFICER MILTON: Of course you wouldn't tell me if you knew, would you? ... You always protect your own kind.

MRS. DESMOND: I take it you're looking for someone connected with the shooting?

OFFICER MILTON: Runs the Western Union office ... Took a shot at a white man last night ... Might even tried to rape his daughter for all we know ...

MRS. DESMOND: You think he might have had something to do with Leslie's death?

OFFICER MILTON: I don't know. Anything is possible.

MRS. DESMOND: Or do you still think it's suicide?

OFFICER MILTON: I still think it's suicide ... But some of the people in this town are beginning to talk up lynching, so I hope I can find this buck before somebody else does.

MRS. DESMOND: You think he's going to be on this train?

OFFICER MILTON: If I were him, I would ... I checked the one going that way ... so I thought I'd try this side of the tracks ...

MRS. DESMOND: I haven't seen anybody ...

OFFICER MILTON: Most likely he'll try to hop it outside of town.

MRS. DESMOND: There's only trouble at one end of the line or the other.

OFFICER MILTON: Look, we have plenty of time ... How about letting me buy you a cup of coffee?

MRS. DESMOND: I don't want to interfere with your official duties ...

OFFICER MILTON: Well I sorta think you're one of my official duties ...

MRS. DESMOND: Well, just one cup of coffee then ... I don't want to take a chance of missing the train ...

OFFICER MILTON: I have a stake in catching this train too ... One cup of coffee and a sinker ...

MRS. DESMOND: And a sinker ... (*As they walk past* MATTIE, MRS. DESMOND *pauses, placing her flowers on* MATTIE'S *lap.*) Don't worry, mother. We'll find somebody to get your suitcase on the train.

Scene One

MATTIE: I'd appreciate that ...

MRS. DESMOND: (*Exiting*) Don't worry, I'm in the hands of the law, so I'll be right back.

MATTIE: I'd really appreciate that ... Yes I would. (MATTIE *removes her telegram from her dress pocket and holds it up to the light. It is still unopened. She smooths it on her lap. While the pin-ball machine continues its whirr of lights and noises,* MATTIE *hums her lullabye.* BLYTHE *enters, looks cautiously around her, and then approaches* MATTIE.)

BLYTHE: (*Whispering*) Hello.

MATTIE: Well, lookey here ... Ain't you a sight for sore eyes.

BLYTHE: (*Whispering*) I was just waiting for them to leave ...

MATTIE: That's right, honey ... You did the right thing ... I guess you got my message.

BLYTHE: Miss Hollandish told me ...

MATTIE: Hush. You let me do the talking. Somebody might be listening.

BLYTHE: Not here ...

MATTIE: When they talk about lynching, everybody's all ears ...

BLYTHE: Yes, ma'am ...

MATTIE: How's your Pa?

BLYTHE: He's in the county hospital.

MATTIE: That's what I kinda figured. Sounds like everytime I turn around lately we're talking about somebody in the hospital.

BLYTHE: They say he's going to be all right.

MATTIE: (*Crosses herself*) Thank the Lord for favors.

BLYTHE: Even my mother's gone down to visit him. (MATTIE *lifts her dress and removes a garter with a key attached to it.*)

MATTIE: You see this? This is the key to Mr. Hall's house ... You go up there and get him these things ... (*Places a list in* BLYTHE'S *hand.* BLYTHE *pockets the key and list quickly.*) That's a list of things he wants. Now you go out to my place and leave them in my barn ... I don't know if he's going to be there or not, but if he's not, he'll be back for them ... But you got to do it before tomorrow night. Otherwise it'll be too late.

BLYTHE: He shouldn't have to run. He didn't do anything ...

MATTIE: Hush. There's no sense talking about things we already know. Now you just get going as fast as you can.

BLYTHE: I've tried to tell everybody. But nobody'll listen.

MATTIE: That's the way some people are.

BLYTHE: They can't do anything to him.

MATTIE: Not if they don't catch him ... You just make sure that nobody follows you ... Now Charley's out there ... So you might as well make sure he's getting fed ... And there's a padlock on the barn door. If Winnie's not there, you make sure the lock's locked, cause I don't want no bum walking in and taking his stuff.

BLYTHE: I will.

MATTIE: Wait ... You'd better take these flowers.

BLYTHE: What for?

MATTIE: It just occurred to my mind that when you came out to my place last night, I didn't give you no tip, and I don't want to leave this town leaving no debts.

BLYTHE: You don't have to ...

MATTIE: I know I don't have to. I didn't read it so I don't think I have to pay for what I don't read ...

BLYTHE: Where did you get them?

MATTIE: (*Indignant*) What do you mean where did I get them? I bought them. Where did you think I got them? I didn't swipe them if that's what you think ...

SCENE TWO

BLYTHE: I didn't think that ...

MATTIE: Get going before they come back.

BLYTHE: Aren't you ever coming back?

MATTIE: I don't know. That's between me and Matthew, and I don't know what my son has to say about it anymore.

BLYTHE: But are you going to be all right?

MATTIE: I have relations in Baltimore so don't you worry your head none about me. You worry about your boss. He's the one needing worrying about ... And make sure you don't lose that list ...

BLYTHE: (*Starting off*) I won't ...

MATTIE: And make him sign a receipt for it ... And just you remember, honey, if the hounds come after you, kick them in the nose. Yes, sir, kick them in the nose real hard.

(*Lights out*)

Scene Four

(*Dream Sequence No. 3. Sounds of a crowd roaring. Squeal of a microphone and then an announcement over a loudspeaker: "And in this corner we have* CHIEF DANCING FOX *in his authentic Indian regalia, and in the far corner in the black tights is the mystery challenger* PHANTOM GORDON, *the man in the cosmic mask." Cheers greet the announcement of each wrestler.*)

(*As the announcement commences, ropes, representing the boundaries of the wrestling ring, are flown in and two wrestlers take their respective places.* CHIEF DANCING FOX, *a horrendous parody of an authentic Indian Chief, removes his headdress and brandishes his tomahawk at the largely invisible crowd, perhaps represented by slides of persons popping in and out. Almost immediately a bell sounds and the wrestlers begin their contest. The crowd roars for blood.*)

ANNOUNCER'S VOICE: "No, sirs. You're not going to find two finer wrestlers in all the world than Chief Dancing Fox and his mystery opponent, Phantom Gordon, The Man in the Cosmic Mask."

(*The wrestling match, a titanic struggle for physical supremacy, continues through the cigar smoke haze for a minute or so, when* BLYTHE *pedals in, pedals down the aisle of the arena, dismounts, and rushes up to the ropes. Again, like the Western Union sign of Act One, the wrestling ring should resemble no other wrestling ring in existence.*)

BLYTHE: Telegram ... Western Union Telegram for Phantom Gordon, Esquire, The Man in the Cosmic Mask.

PHANTOM GORDON: (*In a headlock*) Uaaggh ...

BLYTHE: (To PHANTOM) Excuse me, but are you the interested party?

REFEREE: Kid, what's the matter with you? Can't you see he's busy?

PHANTOM GORDON: Uagggghhhhh ...

BLYTHE: But this is a matter of life and death ...

DANCING FOX: (*Increasing his hold*) You're telling him paleface!

REFEREE: Come on, kid ... Get away from the ropes ...

VOICE FROM CROWD: Get down stupid ...

REFEREE: You're blocking the view ...

VOICE FROM CROWD: Give him a hammer-throw.

BLYTHE: I have to do my job. (BLYTHE *lies down so that she is at eye-level with the man in the cosmic mask who has now been forced to the mat.*) Could you just sign for it as soon as you get an arm free?

REFEREE: One ...

PHANTOM GORDON: Auuarggggh ... Auuughhhhrrrh ...

REFEREE: Hurry up, willya? ... Two ... (DANCING FOX *jumps up and down on* PHANTOM GORDON'S *stomach.*)

PHANTOM GORDON: Uuuaaaaagh ... Uaggggrrrrh ...

BLYTHE: You think maybe I could just read it to him?

REFEREE: O.K. O.K. Just get away from the ropes ...

SCENE TWO

VOICE FROM CROWD: Kill him, Dancing Fox.

VOICE FROM CROWD: Gouge his eyes out.

VOICE FROM CROWD: Stomp him to death.

BLYTHE: It's from your mother.

PHANTOM GORDON: (*Acknowledging*) Aaaauurggghhh ... Auuugghrrrrhh ...

BLYTHE: Just nod up and down if you think it's all right for me to read it. (DANCING FOX *grabs* PHANTOM GORDON'S *face and slams it up and down into the mat.*)

DANCING FOX: What's the matter, Phantom? You no like telegram?

VOICE FROM CROWD: Read it already.

VOICE FROM CROWD: I could have stayed home tonight and listened to Roosevelt.

BLYTHE: (*Singing quickly*) Happy birthday to you, Happy birthday to you, Dear Man in the Cosmic Mask, Happy birthday to you (*And she adds*) And many happy returns of the day ...

PHANTOM GORDON: (*Acknowledging*) Aaaarrrghhhh ... Aauugggghrr ...

REFEREE: Did she send him a cake too?

VOICE FROM CROWD: With a woman in it. But when they got it out of the oven, she didn't look so good ... (DANCING FOX *drags* PHANTOM GORDON *to the edge of the ring nearest* BLYTHE *and he twists his hapless opponent's head into the ropes.* BLYTHE *places the opened telegram on the edge of the ring.*)

BLYTHE: I'll leave the telegram here ... If you look down, you can read it. (DANCING FOX *gives a flying kick to* PHANTOM GORDON. PHANTOM GORDON'S *teeth spit out in all directions.*)

DANCING FOX: There, paleface ... There's your tip ... If you collect the teeth and put them under your pillow, the good fairy will bring you thirty-two dimes ...

54   THE ENVOI MESSAGES

VOICE FROM CROWD: Come on, Man in the Cosmic Mask ... Do something ... I've got a week's salary riding on you ...

VOICE FROM CROWD: Ask him where he got a week's salary from ...

VOICE FROM CROWD: Kill him ...

(*We hear the sound of the bell signaling the end of the round.* PHANTOM GORDON'S *manager tosses a pail of water into the face of the hapless wrestler. His mask begins to shrink.*)

(*Lights out*)

Scene Three

(*As the lights go down on the wrestling match, we hear the voice of* ROOSEVELT.)

ROOSEVELT: (*Quoting Elihu Root*) "'Instead of the give-and-take of free individual contract, the tremendous power of organization has combines great aggregations of capital in enormous industrial establishments working through vast agencies of commerce and employing great masses of men in movements of production and transportation and trade, so great in the mass that each individual concerned in them is quite helpless by himself ...'"

(*We hear the bang of a drum, the sounds of a small political rally in progress. A woman takes her place upon a soap box that is flanked by an American flag on an iron pole. A few torches are lit and are carried by members of the crowd.*)

SPEECH MAKER: Well, you people can sit at home and listen to Roosevelt if that's what you want to do, and if you're naive enough you can believe all the fine things that government is going to do to take care of us, but let me tell you something, I don't see Eleanor giving up any of her fine dresses to clothe me or my children ...

VOICE FROM CROWD: They're not eating beans either.

SPEECH MAKER: That's right. The people who control the means of production want us to go hungry, because the

Scene Three

hungrier we are, the better off the employers are. If you get hungry enough, you'll work for almost nothing and be thankful for it ... that's their philosophy. Eight, nine, ten hours a day for crumbs off the rich man's table. And did you ever ask yourself who gives anybody the right to hire another human being for wages? Who?

VOICE FROM CROWD: The Bible says we have to live by the sweat of our brows ...

SPEECH MAKER: That's right. But we're sweating for somebody else's brow too. Did God give any man the right to own this earth? Can you find a beach to swim on, can you find a lake that somebody doesn't own? I tell you that if we give the millionaires in Washington half a chance they'll buy the sky right from over our heads and charge us money to look up at the clouds.

VOICE FROM CROWD: Can it, sister ... You anarchists are all alike.

SPEECH MAKER: That's right ... You call me names. That'll make everything better. That'll solve all your problems. A handful of people control all the wealth, a handful of people are telling us how to live, where to live, what we have to do with our lives.

VOICE FROM CROWD: Commie ...

SPEECH MAKER: Make up your mind ... Let me tell you why I'm here. I'm here because I don't want you to forget the coal miners in Kentucky and Tennessee, how they wanted to form a union to improve their conditions, and look what happened to them ... They were gunned down like dogs by the capitalist owners ... They'll buy the earth out from under your feet and then sell it back to you by the ton.

VOICE FROM CROWD: You ought to be using that soap box to wash your dishes in.

VOICE FROM CROWD: Let her speak before I bop you one.

SPEECH MAKER: What dishes? I don't have any dishes. And if I had dishes, I couldn't afford to put any decent food on them ... You think we're out of work because it's our fault?

(BLYTHE *enters, but remains outside the crowd.*)

VOICE FROM CROWD: God save the King.

VOICE FROM CROWD: Sez you.

SPEECH MAKER: That's what all the politicians want you to believe ... When something goes wrong, it's your fault ... It's your own lack of virtue ... Did you let the bottom fall out of the stockmarket? I didn't. Did you invent stocks? I didn't. Did you lock the men out of the mills at Lowell, or at the Ford plant in Detroit, or the coal mines in Tennessee and Kentucky? I didn't. No, I swear to god, I didn't. Did you march with the 12th Infantry into Anacostia Flats and drive the Bonus Army into the woods of Maryland? I wasn't with them.

(*A man leaps to the top of a barrel. He holds a coil of rope in his hands.*)

MAN WITH ROPE: I say that she's here to make us forget the real business at hand. I say let's cope with the things we can cope with ... We can't solve the problems in Washington, but we can solve the problems closer to home.

VOICE FROM CROWD: I can't even get my car to work.

MAN WITH ROPE: I say lynch the anarchists. They're the ones leading our country straight to hell in a handbasket ... Anarchists, Jews, Niggers ...

VOICE FROM CROWD: You left out Roosevelt ...

MAN WITH ROPE: And Roosevelt ...

SPEECH MAKER: What's the matter with this town? Everyone's got lynching fever. I say that's what they want in Washington ... They want us divided among ourselves. As long as we're fighting among ourselves, the bastards are squeezing the life from our souls.

MAN WITH ROPE: I say it's time we took the law into our own hands ... Put some people in their place around here ...

(BLYTHE *runs past the crowd and then disappears down a side alley.*)

SPEECH MAKER: Right at this moment, aren't they burning lumber to drive up the cost of construction, aren't the farmers plowing food under and aren't they letting food rot in the silos while we starve?

MAN IN CROWD: (*Displays a brick*) The only thing that stands between me and food is a glass window, and you know what this brick can do, don't you? It opens up a window just as pretty as you please.

SPEECH MAKER: Isn't it time we let Washington know that they can't push the little people around any longer?

(*Lights out*)

(*The sound of a window being broken.*)

Scene Four

(*SCENE: Hotel room at the Ballanger Hotel, perhaps the same room as the one previously occupied by* MRS. DESMOND.)

(*Lying on the bed is the soldier, who at the opening of Act Three was playing the pinball machine at the train station. He lies in semi-darkness, the blinds drawn. Wearing khaki pants and a white undershirt, he lies motionless, his hands folded under his head, staring up at the ceiling. A pile of crumbled newspapers surround his bed.*)

(*There is a knock at the door.*)

PRIVATE MASON: Who is it?

BLYTHE'S VOICE: Western Union.

PRIVATE MASON: (*Not moving*) Slip it under the door.

BLYTHE: I'm sorry, but you have to sign for it.

PRIVATE MASON: Since when? ... Hey, didn't you hear me? Since when?

BLYTHE: I can leave it at the desk if you want ... Mr. Ballanger will sign for it ... Shall I leave it with him?

PRIVATE MASON: All right, do that ... No, just a minute, I've changed my mind ... (*He gets up from the bed, crosses, and opens the door.* BLYTHE *holds out a telegram for him.*) Thanks ... (*He searches his pocket for change, finds none, crosses to the dresser and gathers some nickels and dimes together.*) Come in ... I may have a reply ... Do I have a reply. (BLYTHE *enters cautiously*) Since when do they start hiring girls for Western Union?

BLYTHE: Since me I guess.

PRIVATE MASON: Got pull, huh? ... Well, I guess I've seen about everything now. I'll tell you that when I worked for Western Union there were no girls on the team, I can tell you that. (*Places the change in her hand.*)

BLYTHE: Thanks.

PRIVATE MASON: Don't spend it all in one place ...

BLYTHE: Do you know Mr. Winthrop Hall?

PRIVATE MASON: Nope. Should I?

BLYTHE: Well, you said you worked for Western Union. Mr. Hall runs the Western Union office here.

PRIVATE MASON: Yeah, but I didn't say that I worked here, did I?

BLYTHE: Well Mr. Hall didn't work here all his life ...

(*The soldier tears open the telegram, reads the message to himself, crumbles it into a ball and tosses it across the room into the wastepaper basket.*)

PRIVATE MASON: Two points.

BLYTHE: Do you have a reply?

PRIVATE MASON: Sure, kid, I have lots of replies ...

BLYTHE: My name is Blythe, not kid ...

PRIVATE MASON: All right, Blythe, I have lots of quick, snappy answers, lots of clever songs ... You want to hear my favorite song? ... (*To the tune of the* "Battle Hymn of the Republic", *he sings* "Battle Hymn of the Bonus Expeditionary Force", *a song made famous two years earlier*): "Mine eyes have seen the glory of the coming of the tanks, They rumbled through the

Scene Four

streets behind the infantry in ranks, They were out to save the country for the rich men and the banks, But the B.E.F. lives on! Glory, glory, Herbie Hoover, Glory, Glory, Herbie Hoover, The B.E.F. lives on!''

BLYTHE: Weren't you down at the train station a little while ago? Playing the pinball machine?

PRIVATE MASON: Don't interrupt me when I'm in fine fettle ... Would you interrupt Caruso? Of course you wouldn't ...

BLYTHE: I have to go.

PRIVATE MASON: Wait a minute! What's that ruckus out in the street? All I want to do is sleep my whole life, and everybody is raising holy blazes out my window.

BLYTHE: I think they're anarchists ...

PRIVATE MASON: Anarchists? Well, bully for them ... Close the door will you? I'm getting a draft. (BLYTHE *closes the door.*)

PRIVATE MASON: (*Singing*) "I have seen them put the torches to the shack that we call home, And the flames were red that cast their light on Capitol and Dome, And the mothers and the weeping kids, they turned them out to roam, But the B.E.F. lives on.''

BLYTHE: What's the B.E.F.?

PRIVATE MASON: The Bonus Expeditionary Force.

BLYTHE: (*Knowing*) Oh ... They were talking about the Bonus Army down stairs ...

PRIVATE MASON: Did they mention my name? (*Gives a snappy salute.*) Private Mason, reporting for duty, sir ... Yes, sir, I'd follow General MacArthur right into hell, bayonet fixed, sir ... I'll never forget that day as long as I live ... Hot as holy blazes out there, and there I was in my trench helmet, my bayonet fixed ... (BLYTHE *keeps a safe distance.*) You deliver messages all day, right? Well, you know the message I delivered that day? Tear gas, that was the message I delivered ... Did you ever see four troops of cavalry march down Pennsylvania Avenue, and then there were the men in the tanks ... And hot as holy blazes, did I tell you that? And there were all these old vets who had marched on Washington ... 200,000 of them living out in Anacostia Flats ... Hooverville, that's what it was, that's what everybody called it ... And there I was, a brand new soldier going out to make war. Making war on my own people ... They called us Hoover's Pets, that's what they called us ... But General MacArthur showed them ... They were living in paper boxes and shacks and we set fire to them, and of course the women and children were running like holy blazes, and when the tear gas opened up, mothers would come running out with wet towels thrown over the faces of their babies ... Do you know what it's like to wear a gas mask in July? I bet you don't know, do you?

BLYTHE: (*Opening the door*) I'm sorry, I better go ...

PRIVATE MASON: Children vomiting all over the place. That's not a very pretty sight, is it? ... Is it? Or pregnant women being trampled to death. And they want me to come home and be a big hero ... So go! Get the holy blazes out of here, you with your lousy telegrams. It's no skin off my nose right? (BLYTHE *has left.* PRIVATE MASON *calling after her.*) That's what my life is. One big cuckoo clock. People go in, and people go out ... Right? ... (*He slams the door.*) Aren't you even going to wait for my reply? (*Sings*) "Glory, glory Herbie Hoover, Glory, glory, Herbie Hoover, Glory, glory, Herbie Hoover, The B.E.F. lives on!"

(*He executes another snappy salute and tumbles backward to the bed.*)

(*Lights out*)

Scene Five

(*SCENE: Interior of the barn of* MATTIE TRUERIDGE'S *farm. The barn might be simply suggested by a wagon load of hay and a few deserted animal stalls. Upstage center the barn door, with shafts of morning light sifting through the cracks, is closed.*)

SCENE FIVE

(*Seated on a pile of hay is* MOON MONROE, *a half-breed. Dressed in a black suit that is slightly too small for him, he wears a long black coat and a battered top hat with a single white feather sticking out of it. Like* CHIEF DANCING FOX, *perhaps he too has earned money wrestling, though his long arms and legs seem vaguely disjointed, too long for his body. He quietly plays the harmonica.*)

(*Lying on the ground, on a pile of dirty horse blankets, is* WINTHROP, *dressed in the same clothes as previously, but looking slightly worse for wear. He drinks from* MATTIE'S *molasses jar, but what the jar contains is difficult to say. It is certainly not molasses.*)

(*A rooster rasps outside. In the distance a dog barks.*)

WINTHROP: Goddamn those dogs.

MONROE: Some dogs, some chickens, and a rooster.

WINTHROP: Goddamn some dogs, some chickens, and a rooster then.

MONROE: (*Pocketing his harmonica*) Means someone's coming.

WINTHROP: Might. Dogs have been known to bark without good reason.

MONROE: You said that girl was coming out here.

WINTHROP: If Mattie gave her the message ...

MONROE: Yeah, and I bet she brings a posse with her when she comes.

WINTHROP: You don't trust anybody, do you?

MONROE: (*Crossing to door*) I'd trust another half-breed. After all, a half-breed is a useful compromise. Prevents a person from going to extremes. Keeps him from taking sides.

WINTHROP: Some day you're going to have to take sides.

MONROE: I'm here aren't I?

WINTHROP: See anybody? (MONROE *shakes his head.*)

MONROE: (*Crossing back*) After all, you did try to kill her old man.

WINTHROP: I scared him.

MONROE: (*Agreeing*) You scared him.

WINTHROP: She knows he had it coming to him.

MONROE: What she knows here (*Points to his head.*) she may not know here (*Indicates his heart*)

WINTHROP: Am I suppose to interpret sign language?

MONROE: Blood is thicker than water.

WINTHROP: I think that would depend upon who is doing the bleeding. White man's blood never seemed very thick to me. It seemed to cover everything.

MONROE: Well, then, their ropes are thick and you stay here much longer, we're going to be swinging from a tree.

WINTHROP: Me, not you.

MONROE: You because you're a hot-headed Irishman, and me because I'm here.

WINTHROP: Good a reason as any. (MONROE *picks up a white envelope that has been leaning against* WINTHROP'S *boots.*)

MONROE: I hope this is not your last will and testament.

WINTHROP: Just a farewell note.

MONROE: (*Reading the outside of the envelope.*) Miss Elvira Hollandish ...

WINTHROP: Let me have it.

MONROE: Will she join us?

WINTHROP: No. (*Pause*) She's promised to somebody else.

MONROE: So who isn't? The moment I came into this half-breed world, wasn't I promised to somebody else? My body to the worms, my soul to that great wigwam in the sky. But a promise made is usually a promise broken.

WINTHROP: The one to the worms won't be.

Scene Five 63

MONROE: Maybe she'll follow you to the ends of the earth ...

WINTHROP: No.

MONROE: Did you ever ask her?

WINTHROP: Forget it, huh.

MONROE: When you get to Ireland you can send her a cable.

WINTHROP: No.

MONROE: Why are you so thick-headed?

WINTHROP: I think my days with the dot dot dot business are permanently over.

MONROE: (*Broad smile*) You mean from here on out it's dash dash dash?

WINTHROP: No mad dashes for this sonuvabitch. I've got it all planned out. (MONROE *places his finger to his lips to signal quiet. They listen. There is the sound of someone at the door.*)

BLYTHE: Mr. Hall?

WINTHROP: (*Whispering to* MONROE) It's her. (*The doors of the barn swing back and there is* BLYTHE, *her bicycle parked right beside her.*)

BLYTHE: (*Sees* MONROE *first*) Mr. Hall?

WINTHROP: (*Gently*) It's all right, Blythe.

(BLYTHE *rushes forward and throws herself into* WINTHROP'S *arms. He hugs her.*)

BLYTHE: But are you all right?

WINTHROP: Don't you worry about me.

MONROE: He's fine ... just fine ... (MONROE *starts to pull the door shut.* BLYTHE *jumps up.*)

BLYTHE: Wait! I have my bicycle outside. (BLYTHE *goes out and pushes her bicycle inside.* MONROE *swings the doors shut.*)

MONROE: What did you do with the lock? (BLYTHE *removes it from her pocket.*)

BLYTHE: It's right here.

WINTHROP: Blythe, meet Moon Monroe, a good close friend of mine ... Monroe, this is Blythe Donner ... as in the reindeer.

MONROE: I'm going around to lock us in. (MONROE *crawls out through an opening at the back of the barn.*)

WINTHROP: It looks better if the barn door's locked ... We go in and out the back.

BLYTHE: I brought you everything on the list.

WINTHROP: Anybody see you?

BLYTHE: I don't think so. I left right at dawn and took the back way out of town and circled back.

WINTHROP: Mattie make her train all right?

BLYTHE: I don't know. Everything's really confused in town.

WINTHROP: Everybody still worked up?

BLYTHE: (*Shivering*) Don't you have a fire or anything?

WINTHROP: Don't want anybody seeing smoke.

BLYTHE: Oh.

WINTHROP: So how's your old man?

BLYTHE: He's o.k.

WINTHROP: Just o.k.?

(MONROE *scrambles back.*)

WINTHROP: (*To* MONROE) See anything?

MONROE: Nope.

BLYTHE: He'll be out of the hospital in a couple of days.

WINTHROP: That's good.

SCENE FIVE

BLYTHE: He lost a lot of blood

MONROE: We know. It's not very thick.

WINTHROP: (*To* BLYTHE) It's a private joke.

BLYTHE: Oh.

MONROE: You know why it's so much harder to kill poor people? It's because our skin is so encrusted with dirt that it's difficult for a bullet to get through. It's those clean, scrubbed ones that get mowed down.

BLYTHE: (*Disgusted*) He's going to move back in with my mother.

WINTHROP: Maybe it's for the best. Maybe everything in life is for the best.

BLYTHE: Why does she let him?

WINTHROP: Maybe she still loves him ... Maybe it's something you should ask her.

BLYTHE: I hate him for what he's done.

WINTHROP: No you don't, honey.

BLYTHE: I do.

WINTHROP: Don't argue with me. I'm still your boss.

BLYTHE: Come back to work then so I don't have to do everything myself.

WINTHROP: Don't be too hard on him. He is your old man after all.

(MONROE *checks some of the provisions, removes a box of crackers, and begins eating.*)

BLYTHE: Then why did he say what he said?

WINTHROP: He loves you, that's why.

BLYTHE: No.

WINTHROP: He wants you to be all right.

BLYTHE: He didn't have to lie like that, saying those things about you. I tried to tell everybody what he said was a lie, but nobody'll listen.

WINTHROP: (*Shrugs*) That's the way some people are.

BLYTHE: You can't let them run you out of town.

WINTHROP: I'm leaving of my own free will. I want to be somewhere where I can hold my head high, where I can look people straight in the face.

BLYTHE: You didn't do anything wrong.

WINTHROP: I tried to kill a man.

MONROE: A white man at that.

BLYTHE: But my old man started the whole thing ... You've got to come back with me and we'll tell them.

MONROE: If he sets one foot in that town, he won't have time to tell anything.

WINTHROP: Have you talked with Miss Hollandish?

BLYTHE: I delivered the rest of the telegrams and then got your stuff.

WINTHROP: Put it on the list then.

BLYTHE: I'll do it as soon as we get back.

WINTHROP: (*Passionately*) I didn't lay a hand on you ... She's got to know that. She's got to understand.

(*Embarrassed silence*)

BLYTHE: I wish I had never gone back to that office ...

MONROE: Here, have a cookie. It's easier to face problems on a full stomach.

WINTHROP: You had every right to be there. I always think of Western Union as a home away from home, sort of a place to reach out to the rest of the world from.

BLYTHE: Then you've got to come back ... to keep the office running.

SCENE FIVE   67

WINTHROP: Wire the office in New York and they'll find someone to take my place. I'm not irreplaceable. Who knows? Maybe if you threaten them the way you threatened me that time with all that talk about your uncle, maybe they'll hire you. Who knows? I don't. (*He hands her a list of duties that he has jotted down on a brown paper sack.*) Now I wrote down the combination of the safe for you, and a few other things ... Here, and I'll be giving you my set of keys, since I won't be needing them.

BLYTHE: Where will you go?

MONROE: (*Protecting his friend*) It's a secret ... We're like smoke from a campfire ... We just lift off the earth and disappear.

BLYTHE: As soon as my old man gets out of the hospital I'll make him tell everybody he was lying, just making things up, and he'll get everything straightened out so you can come back again and it'll be just like it was.

WINTHROP: Honey, nothing's like it was anymore. Even the government is falling down around our ears, turning on its own people.

BLYTHE: But what about Miss Hollandish? She'll want to know where you are so she can write you ... You have to keep in touch.

WINTHROP: Blythe, I wanted you to come all the way out here to tell you I was sorry, not so much for what I did, but for what happened ... O.K.?

BLYTHE: It's not your fault ...

WINTHROP: (*Interrupting*) Until you hear from New York, you can handle the messages. You know the code by now. Get Rudy to deliver them, and maybe you can hire somebody else, maybe that Reedy Miller you're always talking about.

BLYTHE: I am not always talking about him.

WINTHROP: Take the money out of the safe and put it in the bank. I don't want them accusing me of taking their money on top of everything else.

BLYTHE: I ...

WINTHROP: Don't interrupt. Now when you go back, look in the bottom drawer of my desk and I think you'll find a couple of bottles of Moxie. I don't know how you can drink that stuff, but if it's what you want ...

BLYTHE: (*Hurt*) You're not even going to tell me where you're going?

WINTHROP: As soon as I get an address, I'll let you know.

BLYTHE: (*Trying to keep control.*) Can I have another cracker?

MONROE: Say cookie.

WINTHROP: (*Pulling on his boots.*) A black man never asks for a cracker ... It's always a cookie or a biscuit or a cake ...

MONROE: At least below the Mason-Dixon line ... I think we better get going.

BLYTHE: They got police watching the train.

WINTHROP: Has nothing to do with us, honey. Monroe and I are flagging down the bus past Miller's place ...

BLYTHE: Let me go with you.

WINTHROP: No. You can't. You know you can't ... Besides you got work to do. There's a lot of people out there wanting to send word about birth and death and marriages, and they're depending on you now.

BLYTHE: Let them find someone else.

WINTHROP: You know the business now. Besides you've got your mother to look after, especially if that old man of yours take it in that head of his to run off with another floozy ... Now you be a good girl and you head on back ... And don't fly like the wind this time. Take your time, go slow, like you're sightseeing, because I want to be on that bus before anyone suspects anything.

MONROE: (*Pointing to the letter.*) Don't forget to give her the letter to Miss Hollandish.

Scene Five

WINTHROP: (*Glares at his friend.*) What letter?

MONROE: The one you spent half the night writing.

BLYTHE: I'll see she gets it ...

WINTHROP: No. I changed my mind.

BLYTHE: I'll explain everything to her.

WINTHROP: It doesn't make any difference. I wrote it for myself, not for her. It's too hard to get people to understand anyway.

MONROE: No sense arguing with that man ... His mother dropped him on his head. (MONROE *places his harmonica to his mouth and begins playing* MATTIE'S *lullabye.*)

WINTHROP: Go out and open up the door. I'll wheel your bike out. It'll be lighter going back than it was coming out.

BLYTHE: (*Tears*) You got everything you need?

WINTHROP: Sure, honey, you did just fine ... (*He gives her a warm hug.*) Just fine. Mrs. Astor has nothing on you.

BLYTHE: I didn't mean for anything bad to happen to you ... I didn't.

WINTHROP: There's no sense talking about that. We know that. We don't even have to think about ... I did it. Nobody else. All you have to do is concentrate on keeping that office spic and span, run a tight ship as my boss told me.

BLYTHE: I'm going to make everybody understand what happened.

WINTHROP: Just get going before somebody finds you here and then Monroe and I will have no chance ... No chance at all.

BLYTHE: I don't want you to ...

WINTHROP: I'm still the boss ... now get ... No fraternization with employees ...

(BLYTHE *scampers through the escape way at the rear of the barn.*)

MONROE: You should give her the letter.

WINTHROP: Maybe I'll mail it.

MONROE: Maybe you will.

WINTHROP: (*Stuffs his letter to* MISS HOLLANDISH *into his back pocket.*) She might not have read it anyway.

(MONROE *returns to his harmonica playing. We hear* BLYTHE *unlocking the door to the barn. The doors swing open and as they do the lights begin to dim. There is a small, single spot on* BLYTHE'S *bicycle. The final image is* BLYTHE *pedalling away furiously. There is the sound of a telegraph key clicking out a message to the world.*)

(*Lights out*)

(*Curtain*)

Mattie's Lullabye

Hush my little baby,
Don't you cry so loudly.
Loud crying will wake
The morning sun
And sun will scorch our land
For what you've done.
So hush my little baby.

Loud crying wakes up the West Wind.
West winds bring us chilly rain.
Chilly rains cause rivers to flood,
And none of us will sleep again.

Hush my little baby,
Don't you cry so loudly.
Loud crying will wake
Up the bossman,
And bossman works us all
Till our arms break.
So hush my little baby.

Loud crying wakes up the landlord.
Landlord asks for room rent.
Paying room rent keeps us poor,
And none of us will sleep again.